THE END OF LIFE AS WE KNOW IT

# CLIMATE CHANGE

## A THREAT TO ALL LIFE ON EARTH

ANNE C. CUNNINGHAM AND KENNETH GREEN



Enslow Publishing
101 W. 23rd Street
Suite 240
New York, NY 10011
USA
enslow.com

*The author wishes to acknowledge the patient and loving encouragement of his wife, Patricia Green, without whose help this book would not have been finished.*
—Kenneth Green

Published in 2016 by Enslow Publishing, LLC
101 W. 23rd Street, Suite 240, New York, NY 10011



**Library of Congress Cataloging-in-Publication Data**

Names: Cunningham, Anne C. | Green, Kenneth.
Title: Climate change: a threat to all life on Earth / Anne C. Cunningham and Kenneth Green.
Description: New York : Enslow Publishing, 2016. | Series: The end of life as we know it | Includes index.
Identifiers: ISBN 9780766072848 (library bound)
Subjects: LCSH: Climatic changes--Juvenile literature. | Global warming--Juvenile literature.
Classification: LCC QC981.8.C5 C63 2016 | DDC 551.6--dc23

Printed in the United States of America

**To Our Readers:** We have done our best to make sure all website addresses in this book were active and appropriate when we went to press. However, the author and the publisher have no control over and assume no liability for the material available on those websites or on any websites they may link to. Any comments or suggestions can be sent by e-mail to customerservice@enslow.com.

Portions of this book originally appeared in the book *Global Warming: Understanding the Debate.*

**Photo Credits:** Cover, Gustavo Frazao/Shutterstock.com; p. 4 Bram van Broekhoven/Shutterstock.com; p. 8 Harry Hamburg/NY Daily News Archive via Getty Images; p. 12 © AP Images; p. 14 Lissandra Melo/Shutterstock.com; p. 18 jaroslava V/Shutterstock.com; p. 20 Beata Becla/Shutterstock.com; p. 28 Georgios Kollidas/Shutterstock.com; p. 32 Hulton Archive/Getty Images; p. 37 FloridaStock/Shutterstock.com; p. 40 Manuel Ocen/Shutterstock.com; p. 46 Daumiu/Shutterstock.com; p. 50 Benjamin C. Tankersley/The Washington Post/Getty Images; p. 52 Debra Millet/Shutterstock.com; p. 56 Carsten Peter/National Geographic/Getty Images; p. 60 Brian Skerry/National Geographic/Getty Images p. 62 SEBASTIAN D'SOUZA/AFP/Getty Images; p. 64 Justin Sullivan/Getty Images News/Getty Images; p. 69 SAUL LOEB/AFP/Getty Images; p. 72 NOAA /Getty Images News/Getty Images; p. 74 LSkywalker/Shutterstock.com; p. 79 Designua/Shutterstock.com; p. 81 Encyclopaedia Britannica/UIG/Getty Images; p. 85 imantsu/Shutterstock.com; p. 88 Felix-Emanuel Catana/Shutterstock.com; p. 90 Mihai.Tamasila/Shutterstock.com; p. 95 Paul Orr/Shutterstock.com; p. 99 ixpert/Shutterstock.com; p. 102 Rex Features via AP Images; p. 106 Piotr Krzeslak/Shutterstock.com; p. 109 artjazz/Shutterstock.com.

# CONTENTS

Energy use by large corporations causes fossil fuels to be released into the atmosphere, resulting in the climate change that we are experiencing today.

## CHAPTER 1

# CLIMATE CHANGE: A MOST URGENT MATTER

**IT IS NOW SCIENTIFIC CONSENSUS THAT THE PLANET** is undergoing rapid and potentially irreversible climate change. In fact, an overwhelming 97 percent of climatologists agree that the temperature of Earth is on a warming track of several degrees Celsius, an alarming trend to which countless peer-reviewed studies have testified at length. Of course, scientists also know that the planet's climate has shifted radically during its 4.5-billion-year existence, ranging from temperatures far too hot to sustain human life to periodic ice ages. Yet what distinguishes our present moment from previous eras is that humanity is responsible for this shift. To put it more accurately, the chief culprit of climate change is an economic system dependent on the burning of fossil fuels for energy and profit.

In 2009 a statement authored by eighteen different scientific organizations warned, "Observations throughout the world make it clear that climate change is occurring, and rigorous scientific research demonstrates that the greenhouse gases emitted by human activities are the primary driver."[1] And while the science backing up this conclusion is incontrovertible, the way forward is anything but clear, raising profound and difficult questions about how, or even if, we are to survive on the planet. One thing is certain: Our window for delay and deliberation has closed, and sweeping action on an unprecedented scale is overdue. A 2012 document titled "Environment and Development Challenges: The Imperative to Act" put this precarious situation succinctly: "Either we will change our ways and build an entirely new society, or they will be changed for us."[2] This stern warning echoed an earlier statement by Gaia theorist James Lovelock, who claimed that "we live on a live planet that can respond to the changes we make, either by cancelling the changes or cancelling us."[3]

To a growing number of writers, thinkers, and activists, most prominently Naomi Klein, author of the groundbreaking 2014 book *This Changes Everything*, climate change is the single greatest challenge humanity will ever face and represents a call to reevaluate not just our individual consumption habits—our "carbon footprints"—but to also consider how society is organized at its most fundamental levels. The unequal distribution of wealth within and between nations, a decrease in rules and controls for corporations around the globe, and massive losses to biodiversity represent only a few of the issues at the core of an emerging movement called climate justice. To those fighting for climate justice, the destructive effects of climate change we are seeing are proof that we cannot accept the path outlined above.

The climate justice movement asserts that since comparatively poorer nations will be disproportionately harmed by the coming adverse weather, industrialized, wealthier nations should step up and assume their fair share of the costs. Western nations should both lead the development of renewable energy technologies and greatly reduce their emissions. Judging by the history of past social movements such as civil rights, if climate justice is to succeed in countering the status quo to achieve any of these goals, it must derive political will from major grassroots support, as the existing power structure will not give in willingly. As we can see, climate change is now every bit as much a political issue as a scientific one. Nonetheless, a basic handle on the history and facts associated with climate change science is a necessary tool for meaningful intervention. The purpose of this book is to provide these facts about climate change, while underscoring the urgency of using this knowledge for major change in our lives and communities, however inconvenient and overwhelming this may appear upon first glance.

## A BRIEF HISTORY OF CLIMATE DISCOURSE

Despite its newfound prominence in the media, climate change is still a fairly young field. As recently as thirty years ago, very few non-specialists seemed terribly concerned with climate change, or global warming, as it was usually then and sometimes still called. For one thing, the threat of nuclear annihilation loomed much larger in the public imagination during the Cold War years. Then, beginning in the 1990s, many climate-related stories started appearing in the pages of newspapers, magazines, and science journals. If the weather turned unseasonably hot, if a glacier was rapidly melting, if spring came a few days early one year, or if a drought lasted longer than normal, the newspapers, radio, and television were quick to run global warming stories. Even then, the headlines were rarely positive. Stories about increases in flooding, drought, forest fires, hurricanes, and disease were linked to evidence that the earth is heating up and that humanity is causing a large part of that change.

At universities, private research institutions, and government research centers, billions of dollars were spent to study climate, defined simply as long-term weather patterns. In 1999 President Bill Clinton proposed spending over $4.5 billion to continue studying global warming and its prevention.[4] Discussion about climate change became the central focus of thousands of scientists, engineers, economists, politicians, business leaders, and students.

Surprisingly, a vocal minority of skeptical scientists and policymakers downplayed the comparative importance of climate change, especially

President Bill Clinton speaks at the White House in 1999 about combating global warming.

in light of other pressing issues such as disease prevention, for example. And some hard-line skeptics denied outright that climate change was even happening. The motivation to aggressively deny climate change is usually fairly transparent, since limits on carbon emissions threaten corporate growth and profits. Moreover, regulatory action undermines the idea that economic growth is the most effective cure for the destructive consequences of climate change. Unfortunately, as Klein and others have noted, this view confuses the root cause of the problem with its solution. Modern capitalism is now on a collision course with any hope of slowing down the rapid heating of the planet. If we wish to rebuild the world community in a more democratic and ultimately sustainable manner, the unchecked power of corporate capitalism must be curbed.

Morality and politics temporarily aside, the drive to scientifically understand the climate is a longstanding human desire. However, as we look back on the past few decades, we see that contemporary climate science and the climate justice movement were both initiated by one particularly powerful season.

## TAKE ACTION!

The transportation of food and goods over long distances is a major driver of fossil fuel emission and, in turn, climate change, but is it always necessary? Attempt to go one week without purchasing anything that was grown or manufactured more than one hundred miles from your home. Shop at your local farmers' market instead of chain grocery stores. What are the challenges to "going local"? What are the benefits?

## THE SMOKING GUN: 1988

In the field of climate change science, 1988 is widely recognized as a critical moment. That year, the weather broke away from normal patterns, starting with an unusually hot spring, moving through a blistering summer, and ending with a strangely hot autumn. Groundbreaking scientists, long aware that human action could change the earth's climate, believed that the weather of 1988 was the "smoking gun" that conclusively tied human activity to the warming of the earth's surface. Ever since that summer, the world has been on "climate watch," with thousands of scientists around the world warning that human activities are causing changes in the earth's climate.

Though the United States (and the rest of the world) had seen heat waves before, 1988 was a big one by anyone's standards. By May of 1988, things were already abnormally warm in many parts of the United States. Record high temperatures were recorded in thirteen cities across the United States. Mild spring temperatures had come to an abrupt end, and the heat of summer was coming on with a vengeance. But a sweltering month of May was only the beginning of the year's weather woes. By June, another sixty-nine American cities broiled under record high temperatures. Energy use soared as people sought escape from the heat in air-conditioned buildings. By July, another thirty-seven American cities found themselves cooking, and there was more to come. In San Francisco, the temperature hit 103°F (39°C) on July 13, setting a new record in the city's history.[5] Thirty-one more cities reached record high temperatures by August. In Los Angeles, the temperature hit 110°F (43°C) in September, causing many people to turn up their air conditioners, sending the demand for electricity skyrocketing. The demand was so high that the city's electrical system could not keep up. Four hundred electrical transformers burned out in a single day.[6] In North Carolina, the heat was so bad during one week in August that it killed more than 166,000 chickens and 15,000 turkeys.[7]

Excessive heat was not the only unusual feature of 1988's weather patterns. It was also an unusually dry year. In fact, the inland parts of the United States had not seen such hot and dry weather for fifty years. But coastal areas felt the heat also, and the drought was still worse in the southeastern United States. Some parts of the country had not seen such dry weather for one hundred years. In Michigan that summer, there was not only a drought, there were also thirty-nine days when it was 90°F (32°C) or higher, breaking a record set during the Dust Bowl days of 1934.[8] The dryness and heat in the summer of 1988 were devastating to farmers. Without rain, crops did not grow as well, producing 30 to 40 percent less food than usual across the nation. The parched soil, normally a fertile planting ground, had turned inhospitable. Even where crops grew, they were stunted. As areas were starved of rainfall, water levels fell in lakes and rivers. Nightly news programs showed pictures of boats stuck in the mud of a shrunken Mississippi River. Cameras panned over vast expanses of parched and cracked fields and giant channels of sunbaked mud that had once been powerful rivers.

It got worse. Before the end of the summer, massive fires broke out in Yellowstone National Park, burning about 36 percent of the park, or nearly 1.2 million acres by August 1988.[9] That was the largest area of Yellowstone to burn in nearly one hundred years. By comparison, in the prior sixteen years, 235 small fires had only burned about thirty-four thousand acres altogether. In mid-September, Hurricane Gilbert, an

A wildfire burns in Yellowstone National Park in the summer of 1988. That year over a third of the park land was burned.

unusually powerful hurricane, caused massive damage in the Yucatán, a peninsula in southeast Mexico between the Caribbean Sea and the Gulf of Mexico. Mexico, Texas, and other parts of the world suffered, too. In some places there were severe floods, as weather patterns dropped too much water on some parts of the world, while the United States was desperately parched. Almost 80 percent of Bangladesh (a very poor country in South Asia) was flooded that summer by the fifth severe flood to hit the country in eight years. And more than three thousand people died in India from a heat wave of historic proportions.[10]

When the worldwide temperature records were studied at the end of 1988, it turned out to have been the hottest year recorded in those areas since humans started keeping temperature measurements more than 120 years before. It was also the fifth year in a row that had hotter-than-average temperatures, making the 1980s the warmest decade in 127 years. The fearsome heat, floods, droughts, and wildfires of that season also presaged climate scientists' dire warnings about what a typical future year will look like if we do not deal with the causes of global warming.

## LINKING THE GREENHOUSE EFFECT TO CLIMATE

The weather of 1988 was like the starter's pistol shot at a track meet, setting off a global race for answers. Why was it so hot? What was causing the droughts? What was causing the floods? What was causing the fires? Possible suspects were quick to emerge.

On only the second day of summer, when temperatures in Washington, DC, had already reached a blistering 101°F (38°C), James Hansen, director of NASA's Goddard Institute of Space Studies, was invited to testify before the US Senate committee on Energy and Natural Resources. Hansen said, "My principal conclusions are; number one, the earth is presently warmer than at any time in the history of instrumental measurements. Number two, the greenhouse effect is probably the principal cause of the current global warmth. Number three, our computer climate simulations suggest that the greenhouse effect is already large enough to affect the probability of extreme events such as summer heat waves."[11]

In linking the warming of 1988 to an increase in the greenhouse effect, Hansen was pointing the finger of blame squarely at humanity. James Hansen was not the first person to link human actions to global weather patterns by any means. But his testimony, coming at the start of 1988's unusual weather, made him a prophet of the global effort to understand climate change.

Temperatures in Washington, DC, were already over 100°F on the day James Hansen spoke about climate change in front of the US Senate committee on Energy and Natural Resources.

Since 1988, human understanding of climate change has improved. Technology has improved our ability to measure how the climate changes day by day, while advances in computer science have improved our ability to explore how the greenhouse effect works. Scientists have long known that certain gases in the air (called greenhouse gases) trap some of the energy from incoming sunlight, keeping the surface of the earth warmer than it would be without those gases. This is called the greenhouse effect, and the extra heat trapping is called global warming. Scientists have also seen that human actions have changed the amount of greenhouse gases in the air, primarily due to carbon emissions stemming from globalized industry, shipping, and transportation.

## THE IPCC'S THIRD ASSESSMENT REPORT

The biggest group of climate investigators in the world was formed shortly after James Hansen's historic testimony. Run by the United Nations, the Intergovernmental Panel on Climate Change, or IPCC, brought together scientists and other climate researchers from around the world to study and write about global warming and climate change. Every five years, the IPCC publishes a massive report that summarizes what is known or suspected about climate change. Their 2001 report, called the Third Assessment Report, is over three thousand pages long and is considered a landmark document in the field of climate studies.[12]

In the Third Assessment Report, investigators conclude that the earth's atmosphere is not only getting warmer but that human action has been causing the recently observed global warming. The IPCC also suggests that other types of climate change have already happened because of the extra heat. But IPCC researchers try to look ahead as well as back, and in the Third Assessment Report, the IPCC investigators predict that a warmer atmosphere will cause more weather like that of 1988. They say that a warmer world will have faster changing weather, with more droughts in some places and more floods in others. IPCC investigators also suggest that changes in the climate will affect animal and insect life as well, forcing some animals to move to cooler areas and causing some animals to become extinct altogether. Other animals, including some insect pests, according to the IPCC investigators, might have to move from their present habitat and shift into new areas, causing disruption among local animal and human populations that are not used to their presence.

Back in 2001, some lingering doubt still surrounded these claims. Skeptics pointed out that not enough was really known about the planet's past climate to know if the sample period of weather under scrutiny was truly abnormal or whether humanity's limited history of weather-watching only made it appear that way. Moreover, skeptical investigators argued that not nearly enough was yet known about the way the earth works to predict what weather patterns might look like even in the near future, much less one hundred or one thousand years into the future, as the IPCC investigators propose to do. While these dissenting opinions provided a valuable check against both incomplete science and possible overstatement of dire predictions, it is now unanimous among scientists that the skeptics were wholly incorrect. The current conversation is about predicting the degree of coming temperature increases, the potential dangers stemming from this heating, and possible strategies to address the problem, both technological and political. That global climate change is under way is simply a given.

As we can see, efforts to understand climate change and the effects that warming will have on the planet and its life-forms are the chief scientific questions of our day because they jeopardize our very survival as a species. Human prosperity in many parts of the world, particularly developing countries, depends largely on the climate. Rainfall, drought, days of sunshine, days of frost, and the potential for severe weather all affect the functioning of human societies and the health of the natural systems they depend upon. Agriculture, tourism, transportation, energy use, and many other activities that define our cities and states are heavily influenced by the climate.

## OUR CLIMATE FUTURE

The quest to understand climate change is different from most other scientific pursuits. While most scientific pursuits take place in laboratories and are worked on by people specializing in only one field of science, climate investigation is a fascinating detective story in which thousands of investigators from different scientific and even nonscientific specialties are trying to answer important questions about the planet on which we live. As the planet heats up, we need to know as precisely as possible how the earth's surface will react to different incremental levels of warming. Does the earth still have natural mechanisms, sometimes called carbon sinks, that can preserve the temperature range in which humans can survive, or will the whole system be pushed off balance and run out of control, to temperature levels that humans would find intolerable?

Finally, ordinary citizens as well as scientists are becoming increasingly concerned with what a warmer earth would be like to inhabit. We know that rising global temperatures will bring about a rise in sea levels, but exactly where will seas rise and how high they will get? These remain open questions. We also know that hurricanes and other violent storms will become familiar events, as East Coast residents who lived through Hurricanes Sandy and Irene can attest. Will all the ice melt at the North and South Poles? How will farming be affected? What about natural ecosystems like forests, deserts, and swamps? Many are now asking what humanity ought to do to prepare for these harsh climate

Stonehenge is a structure that was built in England over three thousand years ago. Some believe that it was used by ancient people as a type of observatory to study the position of the sun, the moon, and the stars.

troubles looming in the future, questions for which no easy answers are forthcoming. Nonetheless, these question must be asked now more than ever.

There is evidence that humanity has long been fascinated with the climate. In ancient times, human beings built many devices to track the change of the seasons. For example, Stonehenge is an ancient monument built in stages between 2800 and 1500 BC in the area now known as England. Based on the position of the sun, moon, and stars sighted over the various stones, Stonehenge could have been used to determine when the seasons were going to change, knowledge that may have been used by primitive farmers to determine when to plant and when to hold religious ceremonies. Since the earliest days of human existence, knowing what kind of weather was coming was vitally important for human survival. Thousands of years after the construction of Stonehenge, humanity is still trying to understand the way the world works and what the future holds in terms of rapidly changing and potentially inhospitable weather.

Weather or climate? The rain, humidity, or heat we might experience on a daily basis is called weather. The pattern of weather over a long period of time is known as climate.

## CHAPTER 2

# THE THEORY AND REALITY OF GLOBAL CLIMATE CHANGE

**IT IS EASY TO UNDERESTIMATE THE REALITY AND** eminent threat of global climate change if we fail to fully understand the key difference between weather and climate. Deniers of climate change science sometimes take advantage of this ignorance, obscuring urgent issues by pointing to one very cold winter as evidence that global warming is a myth. In fact, unusually snowy, protracted winters in certain areas are phenomena directly tied to climate destabilization. But without a handle on basic scientific facts and definitions, one is susceptible to being misled by false information. Thus, a definition of climate, and how it differs from weather, is essential prior to addressing how climate is changing long term.

Weather, as we know, changes from day to day. However, over lengthier periods of time, the notoriously difficult-to-predict daily weather becomes relatively stable, forming distinct patterns that are similar year after year. Those long-term weather patterns are what people refer to when they discuss the climate. Over the short term of decades or centuries, climate stays pretty regular. Most years have similar climate patterns to the year before, and those patterns remain roughly the same decade after decade. Yet as we will explore in chapters to follow, there is a body of solid evidence stating that patterns stable for centuries are already being disrupted by greenhouse gas emissions. Since the atmosphere is a multifaceted system, higher concentrations of greenhouse gases such as methane and carbon dioxide in the air mean more than just higher average temperatures. Because 70 percent of Earth's surface is ocean, higher temperatures yield more atmospheric water vapor due to evaporation. This causes more rain in some areas, and less in others, and potentially disastrous droughts and floods.

Small changes in the weather from year to year are a natural part of the climate system. But there are also long-term trends that are harder to spot. Rather than changing randomly, winters may be colder than average for several years in a row, or summers may be a bit hotter than average for more than one year at a time. Fall might be wetter for several years running, or spring might be drier. And such long-term changes and trends are not always predictable. Evidence from studies of the past tells us that the earth's climate has made some very sharp and unexplained changes in the past. Given that these past shifts in climate were caused by a variety of factors, some unknown, can the currently observed warming trend of about 0.8°C* be conclusively linked to human activity? As we will

**Note: Since the conversation about climate change takes place in Celsius rather than Fahrenheit, all further references to temperature change will be noted in Celsius.*

soon illustrate, the answer is a resounding yes. Scientists are now more interested in predicting just how much hotter the planet is likely to get. Financial and insurance firms are already looking into what the consequences of this future climate scenario will mean for their industries' bottom lines. And activists are strategizing ways to keep warming at the lowest possible end of the predicted range. All agree that our future climate will be much warmer—and our reality more chaotic.

## PLANETARY CAUSES OF VARIATION IN CLIMATE

Granted, not all changes to our climate are directly attributable to humanity. Some natural changeability of the earth's climate flows from the nature of the earth itself, a planet orbiting a sun, in a system with other planets. The earth's orbit, or the path it travels around the sun, is very complicated. One thing that makes the earth's orbit complicated is that the earth does not make a perfect circle around the sun. Rather, the earth swings around the sun on an oval, or elliptical, pathway. That means that sometimes the earth is closer to the sun, and sometimes it is farther away. When it is farther away from the sun, the earth receives less energy from the sun than it does when the earth and the sun are closer to each other.

Another factor about the earth's orbit that affects the climate is that the earth is tilted on its axis, the imaginary line that runs through the earth from the North Pole to the South Pole. That means that sometimes one part of the earth will lean in toward the sun, while the rest leans away. Still another complication is that the earth sometimes wobbles on its axis, exposing different parts of the earth to greater sunlight than at other times. And of course, the earth has a moon orbiting around it.

The mass of the moon causes a gravitational pull on the earth, changing the patterns of water flow in the oceans and changing the patterns of air flow around the earth. Both the air and water flows on the earth's surface move heat around and cause changes in the local weather. On top of all that is a thick layer of unpredictability because of what scientists call "chaos." Chaos is the tendency of complex systems to have undetectable features that can cause sudden and unpredictable changes in their normal patterns of behavior.[1]

Because of these factors affecting the earth's orbit, the planet's climate has always changed over time, putting the earth through many short- and long-term temperature cycles of warmth and cold. At various times in the past, ice ages have dominated the earth, covering huge swaths of the planet in a cloak of massive glaciers and freezing temperatures. At such times, the world was very much colder than it is today. The last major ice age began about three million years ago, and though there have been some short warm periods since then, that major ice age is just now ending. At other times, such as the late Cretaceous period sixty-five million years ago, our planet was a much warmer place, mostly covered in lush jungles and swamps, where dinosaurs such as *Tyrannosaurus rex* roamed the earth.

Of course, human beings were not around to take temperature readings in those dinosaur days. And, even when people did appear on the scene about four million years ago, they did not know how to measure the temperature. That ability did not exist until Galileo developed a type of thermometer in AD 1593. Still, despite the lack of early records, modern scientists investigating the climate have found very interesting ways of estimating what the earth's temperature was like long ago. By gathering a variety of evidence from tree rings and corals, and by taking temperatures from deep inside the earth, scientists have built an understanding of earth's temperature patterns that extend far back before humans were temperature takers. Nonetheless, despite the many mysterious and sometimes sudden changes in climate prior to written human history, we should not conclude that nonhuman causes are driving the accelerated rate of change currently observed.

## CLIMATE SCIENCE, THEN AND NOW

Figure 1 shows the history of Earth's temperature far into the past, as nearly as investigators can puzzle it out from such indirect evidence. Some of this evidence from the distant past, and how investigators gather it, will be discussed later.

As you can see from the figure on page 26, the average temperature of the earth has changed dramatically throughout history. Today's temperatures, while warm, are not as warm as some previous periods. And back in the Triassic and Jurassic periods, temperatures were quite warm by comparison with more recent times. So with all this natural change and climate variation, how and when did we finally figure out that humans are capable of causing global climate change?

The earliest known references to the potential ability of human beings to cause changes in their own climate came from a man named Theophrastus.[2] Theophrastus was a student of Aristotle, the Greek "Father of Philosophy," and studied with him in the third century BC. The observation that got Theophrastus into the science history books was not about global temperature but was about the way that swamps can change local temperatures. Theophrastus noted that when people drained the water

## Figure 1. Earth's Surface Temperature Through History[3]

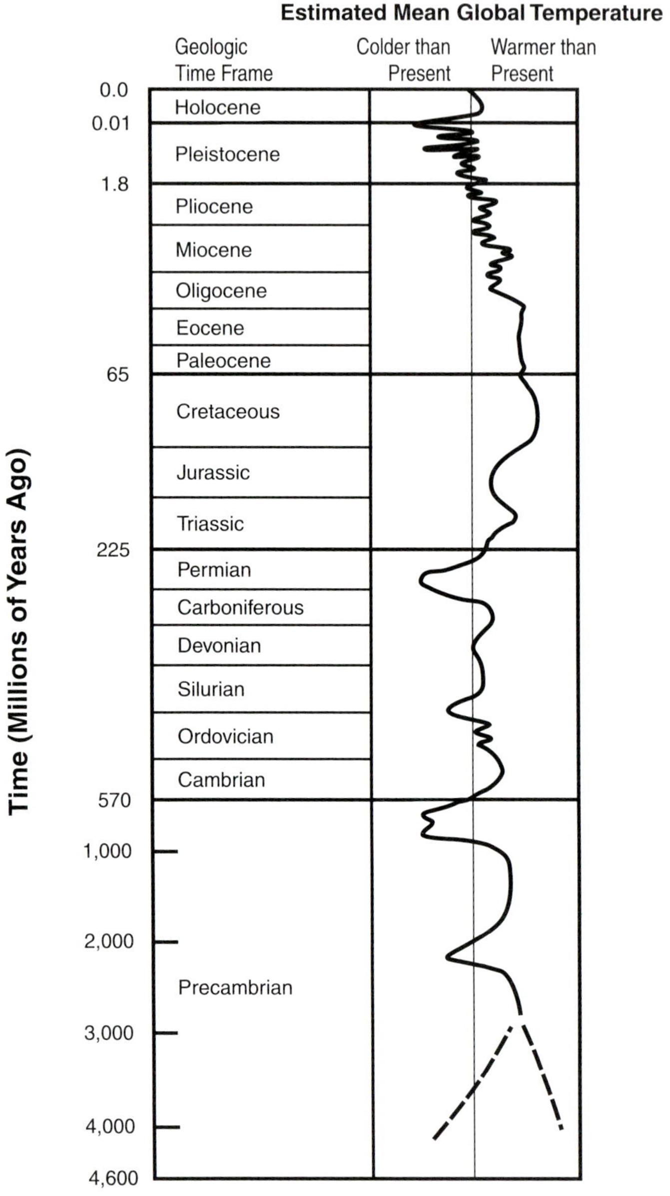


Note: The dotted line in the Precambrian period indicates that scientists are too uncertain about the climate beyond three million years ago to say whether it was warmer or cooler than it is now.

from local swamps (now often called wetlands), the temperature in the local area got colder. Theophrastus also noted that when people removed local forests, the local area became warmer. But in those days, there was little knowledge of how big the world was or how things worked at the level of the entire planet.

Much later in history, in the 1750s, David Hume, a philosopher from Scotland, speculated that the spread of farming had changed the climate of Europe. He noted that the removal of trees and draining of wetlands to allow planting of crops had changed the local climate in Europe. Hume theorized that America, with its rapidly growing agricultural activities, could experience similar change. Still closer to home, Thomas Jefferson, the author of America's Declaration of Independence, also believed that settlement in America would change weather patterns, but for the better. Jefferson believed that settlement in America would tame the harsh climate of the New World. But Jefferson thought that any changes that humanity made to the climate would be beneficial and allow for a more comfortable existence.[4]

These early climate watchers, Theophrastus, Hume, and Jefferson, were talking about *local* changes in the climate. These kinds of changes are well known in our scientific understanding of humanity's impacts on local weather patterns. Today's climate researchers, by contrast, focus first on changes that affect the whole planet and then try to understand how those global changes might cause local climate changes. But today's climate investigators are also looking for answers to other questions. They know climate is warming and will surely cause local changes, so these researchers are seeking more precise answers as to how the climate is changing. For example, what is the extent of human activity's role in the

In the eighteenth century, Scottish philosopher David Hume put forth the idea that human activity could be responsible for changing the climate.

warming that has happened since the 1800s? Did humanity's conversion of forests into croplands have much to do with it? We know beyond any doubt that the persistent and increasing use of fossil fuels is the crux of the problem, but could methane, a gas that is produced when growing rice, also have contributed to warming?

Today's climate researchers are not only looking backward. They need to know how much human activity will change the global climate in the future. Will human activity have moderate, controllable impact on the earth's climate, or might it have catastrophic consequences? Today's climate investigators are looking for the effects that people can have on the earth at all levels, from local to global, through the way they change air that we breathe and the land upon which we live.

## GLOBAL WARMING EXPLAINED

The main theory on which climate investigators base their research is that of global warming. The theory of global warming explains the way certain gases, called greenhouse gases, keep the earth's surface warmer than it would be if the air held less of those gases. Unlike previous studies of global warming that just tried to figure out how the earth's temperature was regulated, the modern theory of global warming focuses on humanity and its impacts. Scientists are struggling to understand not only how the climate works but also how humanity's actions in changing the level of greenhouse gases in the air could be changing the average temperature of the earth's surface.

The theory of global warming has a long and distinguished history, but the most important elements of the theory stem from two very early observations. The first observation is that certain gases can change the way the earth's atmosphere, the layer of air surrounding the earth, retains heat. The second observation is that human beings do things that can change the levels of those gases in the atmosphere.

## EARLY INVESTIGATORS

In 1822 a man named Joseph Fourier investigated the first key observation that rests at the heart of the theory of global warming, which is that certain gases can affect the movement of heat. Fourier was better known as a mathematician, but he also investigated other scientific issues, and studying heat was a strong interest of his. Fourier was especially interested in the way that heat moves from one object to another through space, air, or solid matter. One of the many heat-related questions that Fourier sought to answer was why the air inside a greenhouse stays so much warmer than the air outside it. Earlier investigators had shown that while glass would let some kinds of heat energy such as sunlight pass through easily, it would stop other kinds of heat energy, such as the heat that you might feel coming from a rock that had been heated up during the daytime.[5]

But Fourier wanted to look beyond the glass and see if other forces were also changing the way heat was trapped in a greenhouse. And that led to Fourier's biggest contribution to the understanding of global warming—his theory that in addition to solid things like glass, transparent gases, of the sort found in the earth's atmosphere, could also change the way the earth captures and disperses heat from the sun. Following the scientific method of making observations, then making predictions, and then doing experiments, Fourier demonstrated that his theory was correct. Fourier measured how glass plates would prevent the movement of certain types of heat, all by themselves. Then, using glass boxes filled with either a vacuum or regular air, Fourier measured how heat passed into and out of the boxes. He observed that both the glass and the gas inside were important to regulating the temperature on the inside of the box. From these observations, Fourier concluded that indeed, certain gases in the atmosphere were able to trap some of the incoming heat from the sun and hold it close to the earth's surface.

By modern standards, Fourier's experiments were fairly simple, but his discoveries were big enough to allow later investigators to give substance to the theory of global warming. Still, it was not until the middle of the nineteenth century that the first really convincing experiments were done to demonstrate the heat-trapping ability of atmospheric gases.

In the mid-1800s, an Irishman named John Tyndall took up where Fourier had left off. Tyndall, the son of a part-time shoemaker and constable, went on to study mathematics and science at universities in England, where he investigated the heat-trapping ability of a variety of gases, not just regular air.[6]

In 1859 Tyndall began a series of experiments that would expand greatly upon the ideas of Fourier. Rather than just testing plain air, Tyndall tested several gases, as well as water vapor, for their ability to trap heat. Tyndall showed that carbon dioxide, water vapor, nitrous oxide, and ozone (a gas made up of three atoms of oxygen bound together) could strongly affect the way that heat was trapped in the atmosphere.[7] Tyndall went on to show how some of these transparent gases could trap heat more strongly than others, and he even looked at the way that smog and soot could scatter light and affect the retention of heat in the atmosphere. That phenomenon would eventually bear his name and be called the Tyndall Effect. Tyndall's findings were quite exciting in his time because he did his research in an age when people were not used to the idea that invisible things (like water vapor) could have very strong effects on the environment. Now that people are used to that idea, it does not seem so revolutionary. Back then, Tyndall was breaking new ground.

At the turn of the twentieth century, Swedish scientist Svante Arrhenius published a study in which he explained how carbon dioxide levels in our atmosphere affect the earth's surface temperature.

## BREAKTHROUGH DISCOVERIES: ARRHENIUS

The theory of global warming emerged almost fully formed in 1895, when Swedish scientist Svante Arrhenius suggested that carbon dioxide could function as a greenhouse gas not only to boost the temperature of greenhouses but also to regulate the surface temperature of the entire planet. Noting a correlation between volcanic eruptions and the greenhouse effect, Arrhenius theorized that a lull in volcanic activity could lower the temperature of the planet by as much as 5°C, which could "plunge Earth into an ice age."[8] To prove this, he calculated the cooling effect of cutting in half the amount of atmospheric carbon dioxide. By converse, logic would dictate that a doubling of carbon dioxide in the atmosphere could push temperatures equally far, but in the opposite direction. Arrhenius thus took the next step in thinking about climate, noting that humanity's ability to change carbon dioxide concentrations could lead to changes in the climate we experience year after year. Arrhenius, who was born just when John Tyndall started studying the heat-trapping nature of gases, speculated that this global warming might be beneficial. After all, plants grow better in a warm greenhouse than they do outside in colder areas. Besides putting the finishing touches on the basic theory of human-caused, or anthropogenic, global warming, Arrhenius was the first climate investigator to put some hard numbers to the theoretical relationship between carbon dioxide and the earth's temperature. Remarkably, Arrhenius's calculations have proven quite accurate, especially considering there were no computers in his time. Arrhenius's predictions are still close to current estimates of the temperature-changing impacts of increasing the level of carbon dioxide in the earth's atmosphere.

## RECENT FINDINGS

In Arrhenius's day, the greenhouse effect could be predicted, but not yet observed. However, what began as a theory is now well under way in the real world. In 2014 the World Bank reported that humanity's production of greenhouse gases has already dialed in global temperature increases of about 1.5°C over pre-industrial times, up from the current level of 0.8°C.[9] Mainstream climatologists warn that if current levels of emissions continue unabated, warming will easily surpass the 2°C mark by the end of the century, a threshold long thought to represent the upper limit of acceptability. And the mercury could climb higher still. Kevin Anderson, deputy director of the Tyndall Centre for Climate Change Research warned that a 4°C world is now fathomable, and such temperature increases would show "incompatibility with any reasonable characterization of an organized, equitable, and civilized world community."[10] What's worse, we're already suffering the fallout of a 0.8°C warmer world. An unprecedented European heat wave killed as many as fifty thousand in 2003.

Our increase of atmospheric concentrations of greenhouse gases means more than just heat waves: Hansen and others argue that changing greenhouse gas levels will lead to other climate shifts affecting rainfall. In 2015 California is in the fourth year of its worst drought in centuries, and dangerous wildfires ravage the parched land at the time of this writing. Even more unwelcome changes are predicted as time goes on. In the Arctic and Antarctic regions, oceanic ice is disappearing rapidly. Melting polar ice caps will cause sea levels to rise, although precisely how high is difficult to determine. The 2001 IPCC report predicts a rise in sea level of somewhere between 3.5 inches and 35 inches (9 centimeters and 89 centimeters) by the year 2100.[11] The projected rise is due to both the melting of sea ice, ice sheets, and polar ice caps, as well as the heating of the oceans, which makes them expand. Rising sea levels would swamp some coastal areas and potentially decimate low-lying nations such as Bangladesh. Political instability is a likely result of the mass migration and refugee situations rising seas will cause. Furthermore, when sea levels get higher, the salty ocean water can change freshwater coastal zones to salty or even make underground water supplies too salty to drink.

## CALIFORNIA WILDFIRES AND CLIMATE CHANGE

For several years, California governor Jerry Brown has publicly blamed the wildfires his state is suffering on climate change. The state has been experiencing severe drought, which greatly increases the likelihood for wildfires. "As we send billions and billions of tons of heat-trapping gases, we get heat and we get fires and we get what we're seeing," the governor explained.[12]

One recent report supported the governor's argument. It found that forests in higher elevations, like those found in the Sierra Nevada mountain range, have been burning more in recent years than in past decades. One possible reason is that warmer temperatures are producing more trees but less moisture—a recipe for wildfires.[13]

Going even farther down the chain of cause and effect, some climate investigators have predicted a series of third-hand impacts that might occur as the climate warms and climate patterns change in various areas.[14] They speculate that local animal, plant, and insect populations could be affected by weather changes as well. That could make it hard (or impossible) for some kinds of animals, plants, or insects to survive in their normal habitat. Some species might die off, while other species might migrate into areas where the weather is more to their liking. Biologists have already observed dramatic northward shifts in marine life, a pattern that is consistent with warming oceans. Recently, a blue marlin was caught nearly one thousand miles north of its usual habitat. While this loss of biodiversity is tragic in and of itself, it is also difficult to predict the destructive effects of such shifts. For example, ecosystem movements might lead to people being exposed to diseases carried by insect pests that were previously uncommon to their area.[15]

## TAKE ACTION!

Choose a low-lying island nation (such as the Maldives or Nauru, for example) and research how the citizens of your chosen island are discussing and dealing with sea level rises associated with global warming. How might these perspectives inform our own?

While these predictions are dire indeed, the situation is not without some possibility of relief. The interaction of climate forces leads sometimes to periods of relative coolness. Some of those cooling forces include:

- Heat reflected back into space from the surface of the earth
- Heat reflected upward or downward by clouds
- Heat absorbed and re-emitted by oceans; and more

It was only during the Industrial Revolution, which began around 1850, that the use of fossil fuels increased dramatically, and human impacts on the distribution of forests, prairies, and other ecosystems became widespread. Rather than transition to a sustainable model based on clean

Scientists predict that melting ice caps in the Arctic will eventually result in a drastic increase in sea levels, which would threaten both humans and wildlife.

energy in the years since, we've doubled down on our use of fossil fuels. Although the period from 1850 to the present is but a blip in geologic time, the choices we have made in this time come with dire consequences, as we are seeing. But it is not too late to make choices that bear in mind the fragility of life on this planet.

## CHAPTER 3

# GATHERING EVIDENCE OF A WARMING PLANET

**AS WE HAVE SEEN IN THE PREVIOUS CHAPTER, THE** scientific community has long understood that certain greenhouse gases, once released into the atmosphere by activities such as burning fossil fuels, can affect the earth's climate in serious ways. Moreover, since climate is a very complex, even chaotic, system, seemingly slight increases in global temperature can trigger what scientists call "positive feedback" loops, ramping up the rate of change in dangerous, unpredictable ways.

What began with Arrhenius as an abstract, theoretical pursuit in the laboratory has now become a massive, intergovernmental effort to predict and reign in changes to our natural world that threaten life as we know it. Ever since James Hansen sounded the alarm in 1988, the impending danger of climate change has been public knowledge, yet we have done very little about it. As a nation, we failed to ratify the Kyoto Protocol in 1997 and continue to ignore emissions targets. As individuals, we still drive inefficient SUVs while consuming more and more carbon-intensive goods manufactured overseas. Meanwhile climate change rolls on unabated. How can we do so little while knowing this is happening?

### THE KYOTO PROTOCOL

The Kyoto Protocol is an international agreement in which 141 countries committed to reducing emissions of greenhouse gases. The accord was proposed by the United Nations Conference in 1997 in Kyoto, Japan, and went into effect in 2005. It places a heavier burden on developed nations—those that are most responsible for high levels of emissions. Interestingly, the United States has refused to ratify the treaty, fearing the economic impact of the restrictions.

There are several ways to approach this existential question, most of which fall outside the scope of this book. In this chapter, we will address the difficulties of collecting unquestionable climate change data spanning the entire globe, an enormous area to quantify and measure. Because of these difficulties, climate science has historically been vulnerable to challenges from those whose political and economic interests are threatened by the emissions limits we need to allay the heating up around the globe. To counter such challenges, we need a clear understanding of the methods scientists deploy to collect temperature data, how these data are interpreted, and the confidence that they are accurate. In other words, how have we moved from suspicion that the earth is heating up (and that we're the cause) to solid evidence this is the case?

Climate investigators quickly found out how complicated the job would be when they looked for the answer to the first major question of global warming: Has the temperature at the earth's surface warmed up in an

Fish and animals like the pilot whales seen here could be adversely affected by changes in the temperature of the ocean.

unnatural way in recent years? Actually, investigators had to answer a difficult question even before that. How do you take the temperature of an entire planet? Researchers quickly realized that measuring the temperature of the earth was more than just taking a few temperature readings. In fact, figuring out the average temperature of the earth's atmosphere is incredibly complicated. Calculating the temperature of a large space (such as the oceans, the earth's surface layers, and the earth's atmosphere) is much harder than taking the temperature of a smaller object, or a person, or measuring the temperature of a pot of water.

## TEMPERATURE VARIABLES

How would you take the "average" temperature of the air in a room? You could start by simply putting a thermometer in the middle of the room and seeing what it says. But do we know if the temperature there is the same as near the wall? But if you want to measure against a wall, which wall would be best? And what height on the wall do you hold it against? Do you put it near the ceiling, near the floor, or at the exact middle of the wall? Even small rooms can have major differences in temperature for a variety of reasons. Because hot air rises, for example, a temperature reading taken up by the ceiling would probably be higher than a reading taken down near the floor. You would probably expect a higher temperature reading near the window on a hot summer day than you would against the opposite wall. You would certainly expect a higher temperature reading with the thermometer in direct sunlight than you would if it were in the shade. And if you took a single reading, how much of the room would that reading really represent? Is all the air within a foot of the floor the same temperature? What about the air within two feet of the floor, or up near the ceiling?

To accurately calculate the temperature of a whole room, you would have to take many temperature readings, figure out how much of the room

## TAKE ACTION!

1. Interview a parent, teacher, or relative about climate change. How concerned is he or she? If he or she is not concerned, is it due to distrust of the accuracy of scientific data regarding temperature? Or is it for some other reason?
2. Plant a tree. It may sound trivial, but this activity will literally put you in touch with one of the planet's best defenses against carbon dioxide in our atmosphere.

each of those readings represented, and then use a lot of math to average the many readings of the many different temperature zones throughout the room. As you can see, calculating the average temperature of even a small area is not as simple as it might seem upon first inspection.

Temperature differences based on the location of the thermometer are but one factor. To tell whether the temperature is changing over time, as investigators need to know for climate studies, one would have to take repeated measurements throughout the room and do those averaging calculations time after time. So to see whether that room was showing warmer temperatures over time, you would have to take many repeated measurements. And it is still more complicated if you want to know whether the temperature readings you are taking are abnormal for that particular time of year. In measuring that room, you would also have to pick times that reflect the overall pattern of temperature change and not pick times that only show extremes like the hottest minute or the coldest one.

Trying to calculate an average temperature and track how it changes over time would pose a serious challenge even for a single room. And such a measurement would still only tell you part of the story; it would not reflect the way the heat of objects within the room might change, such as the walls, the floor, the ceiling, or the desks. It would not tell you how the plants, animals, or people in the room would react to the changing temperatures either. And even knowing the temperature, its trend, and its "normality" would not necessarily tell you the best way to change things more to your liking.

When you consider the complications in figuring all this out for just one room, it becomes obvious that it is far more difficult to prove the earth is warming than to merely assert it. Furthermore, to conclusively link global warming to human action, the data must clearly demonstrate that greenhouse emissions are the primary factor in all observable temperature increases over time. Otherwise, warming could be attributable to any other natural factor causing variation in the planet's temperature.

It is tricky enough to take the planet's temperature. But to prove that temperature changes observed over time are consistent with rising levels of greenhouse gas in the atmosphere, multiple sources of accurate temperature data are a prerequisite. Luckily, for over 150 years, people have taken temperature readings at different types of weather stations, giving climate investigators four main sets of temperature readings to work with in looking at the trends in the atmosphere's average temperature. The four sets consist of temperature readings taken at weather stations on the ground, on ships at sea, from floating weather balloons, and by satellites orbiting the earth. Despite the difficulties in gathering these data, we can rest assured they are accurate, and most discrepancies have been accounted for mathematically.

## METHODS OF TAKING THE EARTH'S TEMPERATURE

The biggest set of temperature readings investigators use to study the warming of the atmosphere are taken using regular glass thermometers at land-based weather stations. Until the recent development of electronic thermometers, these readings were taken with the same kind of glass thermometers people use to measure the temperature of the air in their living room or the water in a pool. Currently, there are millions of individual temperature measurements being taken every year using regular glass thermometers at over eight thousand weather stations all around the world.[1]

The process of joining all those temperature readings together and calculating an average global temperature is a huge challenge. As discussed earlier, for even a single room, you would have to make assumptions about how much of the room a given thermometer reading really represents. With its widely varied temperature zones and patterns, the earth's surface is many times more complicated than a single room.

Figure 2 shows how the earth's average temperature has changed over the last 150 years. Since the temperature of the atmosphere can fluctuate by more than 50°C in a single day at some spots on the earth, climate investigators perform a calculation that lets them express an area's temperature by the way it differs from the average temperature for that time and place observed over a long span of time, such as thirty years. These values are called "temperature anomalies." Temperature anomalies do not represent the actual temperature; they just say whether the temperature was warmer than average or colder than average for the time the measurement was taken.

Climatologists argue that the trend shown in this graph indicates that the earth's atmosphere has warmed up over time. In their last published report, IPCC investigators said their research indicates that temperatures recorded at measuring stations on the ground reveal an average warming ranging from 0.4°C to 0.8°C since the year 1850. That is, the average temperature of the atmosphere near the earth's surface in the year 2000 was between 0.4°C and 0.8°C warmer than it was during the year 1850.

One half to one third of this warming, according to the investigators, has happened since the mid-1970s. But the IPCC investigators point out

Figure 2. Global Annual Temperature Anomalies, 1850-2010[2]

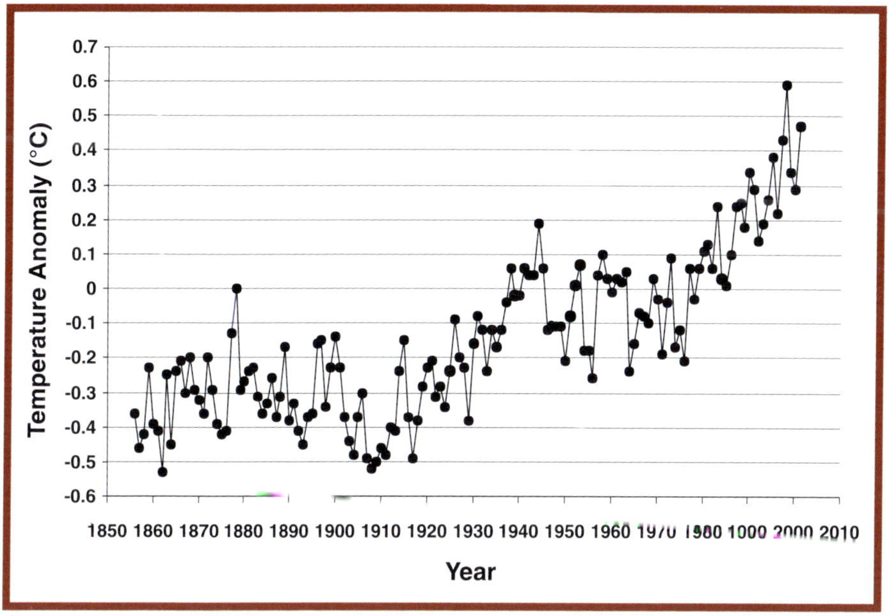


that the warming of the earth's average temperature has not caused a uniform amount of warming to happen everywhere around the earth. Some parts of the earth have warmed up more than others. For example, more of the warming seen since 1850 has happened over land rather than over water. And the warming is not spread out evenly over the course of the day or night. In fact, more of the warming seen since 1850 has happened at night. The warming also shows up mostly during an area's winter. So, instead of making for warmer summertime days, the warming since 1850 has made mostly for slightly warmer wintertime nights. Finally, more of the warming since 1850 has happened over the high-latitude parts of the earth, particularly in the north, rather than over areas closer to the equator.

Some scientists have pointed out that 150 years worth of temperature records is a tiny sample, given that the earth's climate has been evolving

Temperature readings are taken at thousands of weather stations around the world, like this one on a mountaintop in Germany. The data help scientists who are trying to calculate trends in climate change.

and changing for four billion years.[3] To understand how short a stretch of history 150 years is, consider this thought experiment. If you squeezed all of the earth's history into a single twenty-four-hour period, humanity's direct measurement of the temperature would only cover the last three one thousandths of a second. That is far less time than it takes for the blink of a human eye. Even one thousand years of temperature readings would equate to only two hundredths of the last second.[4]

And then, as some climate investigators have observed, many of the temperature records suffer from accuracy problems. Thermometers used in taking older recordings were primitive by modern standards, some even having hand-painted number scales. And since the people taking the temperature readings were not all working together, they did not collect temperatures in a way that would shed the most light on the temperature of the entire earth. For one thing, not all the temperature readings were taken in the same way. Some readings were taken in the sun, while some were taken in the shade. In some cases, the thermometer was moved around; in others, it was always in the same position. Some weather stations only recorded the temperature for a short period of time, while others recorded for longer.

One possible problem with the record of temperatures taken on land is that most of the readings were taken near cities, and cities, as Hume pointed out, can change the local temperature all by themselves.[5] Hume had not identified the different factors that cause a city to be warmer than the surrounding countryside, but modern scientists have. Because they have fewer trees to shade them and more dark-colored paved surfaces, cities tend to absorb heat during the daytime more than surrounding, less developed areas do. This effect, called the "urban heat island" effect, is what keeps a city warmer than the countryside around it. While critics of climate science have cited the urban heat island effect to challenge the accuracy of temperature records, IPCC investigators have corrected for this effect through various means. Thus, the surface temperature record is an accurate reflection of temperature changes that have occurred over the last 150 years.

## OTHER METHODS OF MEASURING TEMPERATURE

Temperature readings of both the water and the air were also taken on ships traveling the oceans, for a variety of uses. These temperature records span nearly the same time as the land-based readings, but for many reasons they are not as useful for charting the earth's temperature as the land-based readings.

It is even more complicated to take the temperature of the air when you are on a ship at sea than it is when you are on the ground. For one thing, until very recently, ships did not know their exact locations on the surface of the earth, unless they were in a port. Once a ship took to sea and went beyond the sight of land, ship captains could record their position on the globe only roughly, by calculating their latitude and longitude. That inability to know exactly where they were is important because the temperature of the earth changes from place to place, even over the ocean and even over only a few dozen miles. And there were other complicating factors as well. As climate researchers found when they started looking into the accuracy of ocean-based temperature readings, the changes in technology were even more dramatic at sea than they were on land. Before 1940, for example, ocean water temperatures were taken by having sailors pull buckets of water out of the ocean. Sailors would then stick a thermometer in the bucket and take the temperature of the water while the bucket was sitting on the deck of the ship. Investigators looked at these recordings partly to learn about the temperature of the water itself but also to learn about the temperature of the air above the water.

Complications arose right away. As sailors pulled the water bucket up and left it sitting on the deck of the ship, the temperature of the water could change depending on whether it was cloudy or bright, windy or still. And if the bucket was put in a shaded place, it would cool faster than in a sunny place on deck. Even the direction the ship was traveling in could change the temperature readings, because the wind might blow differently depending on which way the ship was pointed with respect to the wind. But those were only the obvious problems investigators found with the temperature readings. When looking still further, scientists found that the temperature reading of the water also changed depending on what kind of bucket was used. When pulling the bucket of water up out of the ocean, air flowing by the bucket would chill the water inside. This evaporative cooling is how some types of home air conditioners work, and it is also how your body cools down when you sweat and stand in the breeze. Climate investigators found that if the bucket the sailors used was made with canvas, this evaporative cooling effect would be greater than the cooling that would happen if they had used a metal, wood, or plastic bucket.

Similar problems affected the normal air-based temperature readings taken on ships. As with water temperature readings, air readings were not always taken at the same places on the earth. But even where they were, there was a problem. Because the ships themselves got bigger over time, the sailors standing on the deck recording the air temperature were actually taking temperatures farther above the surface of the ocean than previous sailors had, even if they were in the very same place.

Climate researchers have some more modern sets of temperature recordings taken since the 1960s, when some high-technology approaches to tracking the weather became more commonplace. Since the 1960s, for example, temperatures of the air have not only been taken at ground level, but they have also been taken with thermometers and other temperature-measuring devices mounted on weather balloons. But even these modern records are limited in the information they tell climate researchers about the global temperature.

The biggest limitation of weather balloons, like that of surface temperature readings, is that they only measure the temperature over certain parts of the world, namely, where weather stations sent them up. Though

A meteorologist in Virginia prepares to release a weather balloon. These balloons can be used to track air temperature as well as other weather-related information.

they do drift away from where they are launched, balloons have not been sent up to all parts of the atmosphere evenly nor over extended periods of time. Balloons were used, originally, to detect local temperatures in order to predict short-term weather, not long-term trends in the climate. Thus, depending on what kind of information was most desired, balloons were sent up to different heights, were kept up for different periods of time, were flown at different times of the day or night, and were flown over only a tiny fraction of the earth's surface, namely, where people lived and had weather research stations. Further complicating things, balloons also had different kinds of thermometers and radio equipment used at different times and places, making temperature readings hard to compare with each other.

The most recently assembled, and most high-tech, set of direct temperature readings comes from satellites that orbit the earth. These satellites record the temperature of the atmosphere using special cameras that measure the heat given off by the upper layers of the earth's atmosphere. Satellite temperature readings are the first ones that can actually measure the temperature of the entire atmosphere at different heights. Such global satellite temperature readings have been taken nearly continuously since 1979. Still, as some climate investigators point out, the satellite temperature readings have their shortcomings. Just like land-based and ocean-based temperature recordings, satellite recording devices have changed over time. Newer devices do not measure the temperature in exactly the same way as previous devices did. Furthermore, satellites do not stay in orbit forever. Eventually, the satellites spiral down toward the earth and burn up in the atmosphere. Indeed, when they looked more closely, climate investigators found that the temperature readings taken by satellites

Weather satellites like the one shown here can provide us with temperature readings at many different levels of the earth's atmosphere.

change as they slowly spiral in toward the earth. Because of the way the satellites take the temperature of the atmosphere, the readings depend on how far away the satellite is from the earth. Temperature readings taken from closer into the earth are lower than readings of the same place on the earth's surface when taken from a higher orbit.

Aside from technology changes, climate investigators differ over the real meaning of land-based, water-based, satellite, and balloon temperature recordings. As discussed above, it is hard to know what the slight warming seen in the temperature records taken on the land really means, because the land-based temperature record is so short compared to the long history of the earth's climate. Temperatures taken

Figure 3. Temperature Anomalies from Surface[6], Satellite[7], and Weather Balloon[8] Measurements, 1978–2002

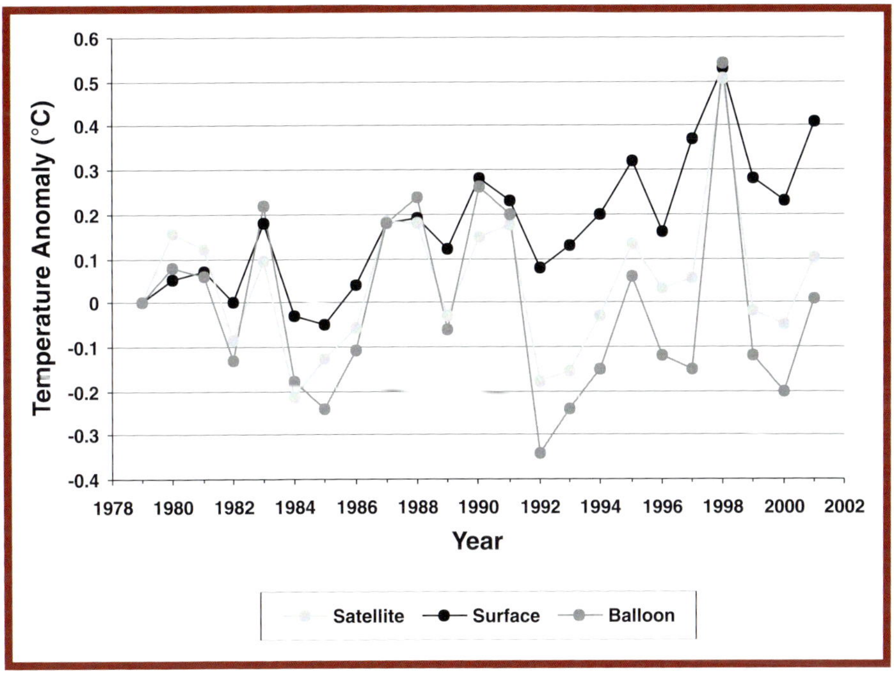

from weather balloons and satellites span an even shorter period than the surface temperature readings or ocean temperature readings do. Further complicating the picture is the fact that the newest temperature readings from satellites and balloons do not tend to match up well with the readings taken on the land or at sea. While the surface and ocean temperature records tend to match up pretty well with each other, and the satellite and balloon temperature readings match up with each other, the readings taken from higher up disagree with the readings taken near the earth's surface. Figure 3 shows how the three main sets of temperature recordings match up over time.

At first, satellite and balloon evidence seemed to suggest that little or no warming had happened higher up in the atmosphere. John Christy, a climate investigator who takes such satellite readings, claims that if the scientific theories used to understand all of the complicated climate processes on earth are correct, then the satellite readings should not show a cooling trend. Christy argued that the disagreement between the different temperature records means there is something missing in the basic theory of global warming.[9] However, in a report by the United States National Academy of Sciences (NAS), a highly respected panel of investigators argued that the difference between ground, balloon, and satellite measurements does not indicate a real problem with global warming theory. The NAS argues that while the surface and satellite temperatures disagree with each other and with some of the theories of how the earth's climate really works, the differences in the two temperature records do not mean that either of them are wrong, only that science has not yet explained why they could differ.[10]

## BOREHOLES AND ICE CORES

Climate investigators studying global temperatures would have a harder job if the only evidence they had was the direct temperature readings discussed in the previous section. For one thing, they would be stuck with only 150 years of data, from which they would be trying to understand trends lasting hundreds or thousands of years. Fortunately, there are ways to estimate past temperatures, even though nobody was around to take measurements at the time.

Climate investigators can estimate the temperature from the past, before there were temperature readings to rely on, through the examination of something called a borehole. A borehole is made when scientists bore a deep cylinder-shaped hole in ice, soil, or mud. Scientists can use such holes to estimate what the temperature must have been long ago. And by studying the long cylinders of ice that can be pulled out of glaciers (called ice cores), scientists can learn even more about the climate of the past.

Climate investigators have found that boreholes can be used to estimate temperatures from long ago, because heating and cooling of things follow predictable trends over time. If you think about it, things do not heat up or cool down all at once; it takes time. Even things like soil, rock, and ice heat up and cool down over time in a predictable way. So how do scientists tell the temperature of the past by looking at the inside of a hole? They do it by understanding that glaciers, and the other solid surfaces on the earth, were made more recently than the parts deeper down. Just as you dig down in the earth to find fossils and things that lived long ago, so scientists can dig down into the earth and find out what the temperature was at times in the distant past.

After drilling a borehole into a glacier, a lake bottom, or regular soil, scientists lower sensitive thermometers into the hole and measure the temperature at different depths. For ice, for the muck at the bottom of a river, and even for regular soil, deeper layers are a reflection of the past, and they can be used to estimate the temperature of the surface at that time. By examining the fossils found at those different depths, climate investigators can estimate which depth matches up with a certain time in the past and can estimate what the temperature was thousands and even hundreds of thousands of years ago.

Over six hundred such boreholes have been drilled around the world in efforts to chart what the local temperatures were before humans started taking measurements with thermometers. By pulling tiny bubbles of air out of the ice cores from depths matching up with times in the past,

Scientists in Antarctica drill into ice for a core sample. These ice cores provide information on the climate of the past.

climate investigators can measure the types of gas found in the atmosphere at the time, including the greenhouse gas carbon dioxide. With such information, climate investigators can not only study the temperature but can also track how past temperatures match up with historical levels of carbon dioxide and use that information to test the theory of global warming. Most such studies of ice cores suggest that higher levels of carbon dioxide happen nearly at the same time as increases in temperature, but some studies suggest that it is not always so.[11]

Climate researchers studying temperature measurements taken from boreholes suggest their findings agree with the thermometer readings of the last 150 years and show the warming goes a bit further back as well. Their findings indicate that the earth's atmosphere is growing a bit warmer and has increased in average temperature by about 1°C over the last 150 years.[12]

When scientists estimate ancient temperatures from boreholes, they have to be very careful that the holes were not contaminated during the drilling process, and they have to make many assumptions. They make assumptions about how fast heat travels through ice and about whether gas bubbles retain the same concentrations of gases that they had so many thousands of years ago.[13] As the IPCC's report points out, many things can interfere with the relationship between ice core readings and the actual surface temperature. For example, when humans change the environment, replacing natural land cover of shrubs or trees with planted crops, for example, they can cause changes in the winter snow cover and soil moisture of areas nearby. The same is true when people build cities where there once were prairies, forests, or swamps. And over time, as human societies moved around, the changes they made in the environment could make the borehole temperature readings less accurate. And other investigators have pointed to deeper problems with information gathered from ice cores and boreholes. The biggest riddle is that sometimes the temperature seems to match up with carbon dioxide levels, and sometimes it does not. If carbon dioxide were causing global warming, we would expect the carbon dioxide level to rise first and then the temperature to rise second. But studies of ice cores show that sometimes the temperature and carbon dioxide go up in tandem, yet at other times carbon dioxide goes up first, and the temperature increase lags, by up to one thousand years. Sometimes, the temperature goes up first, and the carbon dioxide follows. Scientists have yet to account for every question about the distant past brought up by ice cores. However, the evidence still supports a link between increased atmospheric concentration of carbon dioxide and warming.

## TREE RINGS

The way trees grow depends on many different things, but one important factor is the temperature. Trees grow faster when it is warm than they do when it is cold, and as they grow, trees produce "rings" that preserve information about how warm or how cold it was during a given growing season. Because trees grow differently based on local climate conditions, tree ring records say more about local changes in climate than they do about the earth as a whole. Climate investigators looking at tree rings have estimated what the temperature was as far back as the oldest living trees, all the way back to AD 1000 for some tree species.

While they contribute to the big picture, tree ring records are only of limited use to climate investigators. For one thing, trees grow only on land, and they have to be quite old to tell investigators about the temperature of the more distant past. As climate investigators have found, trees that big and old are not very plentiful. And even when the right tree is found, tree-ring patterns can sometimes lead to false conclusions about the local weather. Out by the coast, for example, ocean currents and other climate factors can produce local temperatures that are not always reflective of the region as a whole, so figuring out whether the tree rings really represent the temperature of a significant area is tricky. And then, tree-ring evidence poses many other problems for climate investigators, since the rings represent not only temperature but also rainfall and other factors.[14]

## CORALS

Still another place that climate investigators look for information about past climate conditions is out in the oceans—or areas that used to be oceans. Climate investigators have found that when shell-bearing ocean animals (such as coral) make their shells, the minerals they use vary with the temperature of the water. The temperature of the water, in turn, is related to the temperature of the air. Corals are tiny invertebrates that build their shells on top of the shells left behind by earlier shell-makers. Because the minerals used in making those older coral shells reflected ocean conditions at the time, they are like little recordings of what ocean conditions and temperature were at the time they were made. Since corals grow upward, toward the light, older layers are farther down in the ocean. By looking at the different elements incorporated into ocean coral (and the bands of color that match up with past periods of warmth), climate investigators can estimate the temperature of the water from thousands of years in the past.

In general, evidence about past temperatures from the study of corals matches up well with tree rings in estimating past temperatures, and

These scientists are examining samples from a coral reef in order to learn how it has been affected by climate change. Studying coral can also give researchers valuable information about the past climate of the ocean.

both temperature histories suggest a recent global warming. But as with tree rings, there are limits to the usefulness of coral-based temperature estimates. While temperature is one factor involved in the way that corals build their shells, other factors are also involved, such as the saltiness of the water, the presence of nutrients that corals need to build their shells, and the presence of other minerals dissolved in the water. Diseases and long-term ocean current patterns like El Niño and La Niña can strongly affect coral growth patterns as well. And, like tree rings, corals are not distributed evenly around the world, and those useful for taking temperature readings are from selected places and may not reflect the temperature of the rest of the earth very well.

## CHAPTER 4

# HAZARDOUS EFFECTS OF CLIMATE CHANGE

**EXTREME WEATHER EVENTS AND CLIMATE-RELATED** news stories trigger in us a gut feeling that climate change is an issue we must take seriously right now. While this is a great starting point from which to build awareness, we must be informed by more than just intuition. To that end, we have become acquainted with scientific thinkers theorizing exactly how human activity affects the climate and seen the proof of this as it played out in the real world. We have also countered the familiar doubt expressed by climate-change skeptics such as novelist Michael Crichton and others (If they can't predict the weather for next month, how can they predict the climate a hundred years from now?) by explaining the difference between localized, short-term patterns called weather and long-term trends known as climate. And to instill confidence that our data are correct, we have taken an in-depth look at several methods of gathering temperature records, all of which show that the globe has heated up around 0.8°C in the past 150 years.

Weather events like the 2004 floods in Mumbai, which caused hundreds of deaths, may be a symptom of the rise in atmospheric temperature.

We are already seeing the effects of this seemingly tiny temperature increase, which is but a hint of what's to come—if we do not act. From the elderly Parisian casualties of a 2003 heat wave, the victims of a 2004 flood in Mumbai, to Californians now living through the most intense drought in centuries, few will escape our hotter and increasingly volatile future unscathed. And the damage is not limited to humans. As Elizabeth Colbert has documented in her 2014 book *The Sixth Extinction: An Unnatural History*, loss of species biodiversity never before witnessed is also under way. Taken together, all of this is more than just a body of "circumstantial evidence" proving climate change is real. Rather, it represents a moral imperative to rethink our economic system, reduce our reliance on fossil fuels, and remedy the disproportionate harm poorer nations will experience as a wild and unruly climate future becomes the present.

## "A HARD RAIN'S A-GONNA FALL"

In addition to the "sad forests" and "dead oceans" predicted in Bob Dylan's 1962 ballad "A Hard Rain's A-Gonna Fall," the folk singer's heavy precipitation is certainly coming to pass as well, albeit in unpredictable ways. According to climate change theory, increased temperatures will speed up the cycle of evaporation and rainfall that scientists call the hydrologic cycle. That increased speed leads to increased rainfall, causing floods in extreme cases. Of course, not all areas would experience the same thing, because many different forces control rainfall, including wind patterns, humidity levels, and the shape of the land. The coming "mega-droughts" scientists are predicting too have much to do with this phenomenon.

IPCC investigators report that trends in rainfall have been mixed. Though more than twenty thousand weather stations have recorded rainfall levels, the fact that the earth is 70 percent ocean makes trends in rainfall hard to spot. Over land, IPCC investigators think that rainfall has increased by about 2 percent since the beginning of the twentieth century, but the distribution of the change has varied around the earth. During the twentieth century, for example, rainfall increased between 9 percent and 16 percent over the parts of the earth above the equator, from 35°N to 85°N latitude. During that same time, rainfall levels increased between 2 percent and 5 percent in the band below the equator, from 0°S to 55°S latitude. Rainfall over the United States has increased between 5 percent and 10 percent since 1900, but there have been long periods of drought as well, such as those during the 1930s and 1950s. Over Canada, rainfall has increased over 10 percent during the twentieth century, while over China, the last fifty years have seen a decrease in annual rainfall. Over the area that used to be called the Soviet Union, rainfall has increased over the twentieth century. Like the temperature trends discussed above, changes in rainfall are happening unevenly both geographically and over time. Complicating the situation, the places receiving more or less rainfall do not necessarily match up with the places experiencing temperatures that are warmer or cooler than average.

Besides serving as evidence of global warming, tracking rainfall patterns is important for another reason: If the earth is warming up, harmful consequences will be tied, in large part, to changes in rainfall. Floods,

In 2015 Lake McClure in Coulterville, California, was at 7 percent of its normal capacity. The drought conditions across the state are some of the most severe in history.

droughts, and even very heavy rains significantly interfere with activities such as farming, construction, and transportation, cause massive property damage when cities and towns are flooded, and can kill people. But IPCC investigators note that records of rainfall, while accurate, are not yet perfectly free of errors. They point out that records of rainfall cover only certain areas for certain periods of time, are not always taken with the same accuracy or equipment, are subject to changes because of the wind, and do not always have information about the extent of rainfall in the area around the rain gauge.[1]

## SEA LEVELS ON THE RISE

Global warming theory asserts that rising global temperatures cause sea levels to rise because water expands more when it is hot than when it is cold. On top of that thermal expansion, melting glaciers, snow packs, and parts of the polar ice caps now on the land would add water to the oceans and raise the level as well.

As glaciers have melted since the last ice age, the seas have risen dramatically. Since the last glacial maximum (18,000 to 22,000 years ago, when glaciers covered much of the earth), sea level has risen by over 394 feet (120 meters) at locations near and far from the now-melted glaciers. Investigators have also shown that the sea level rose sharply between fifteen thousand and six thousand years ago, when they rose at an average rate of a little over 4 inches (10 millimeters) per year. Sea level rise slowed down somewhat from six thousand to three thousand years ago, only rising at about 1/16 of an inch (about 0.4 to 0.6 mm) each year, and from about three thousand years ago until recently, sea level rise was slower still, at only about 0.1 to 0.2 mm per year.[2]

Recent amounts of sea level rise might not seem like a lot, but small changes in sea level can mean big trouble for people and animals living in and near the ocean. Not only can rising sea levels flood coastal properties, they can also force salty ocean water underground, contaminating local freshwater supplies and changing the saltiness of freshwater estuaries, affecting local fish and bird populations. And rapidly melting Arctic sea ice threatens the natural habitat of wildlife such as polar bears.

Some recent studies of sea levels indicate an increase in the rate of sea level rise, estimated to be between 4 and 8 in (10 and 20 cm) over the last hundred years. However, there is some doubt attached to that figure, because the land also rises and falls due to underground activity, and ocean currents change as well. Adding to the confusion is the fact that because sea level changes so slowly, short-term records are not as accurate as long-term records. And different parts of the earth's oceans rise at different rates because of their underwater landscape, further complicating the picture. Finally, several trends have climate investigators scratching their heads. For some parts of the world, such as Antarctica and Greenland, evidence suggests that the level of the ocean has actually dropped.[3] And though the rate of global warming has been speeding up, there is little evidence that the rate of sea-level rise has sped up to match, as theory would suggest. Though warming and glacial melting have both sped up in the twentieth century, the sea level did not rise at a faster rate in the twentieth century than in the nineteenth century.[4]

Due to the complexity and difficulty of measurements, precise predictions of the coming rise in sea level are elusive, but we can be sure it is happening. The IPCC predicts that sea level will rise by between 3.5 and 35 in (between 9 and 89 cm) by 2100. Although the midpoint of 19 in is not enough to destroy US coastal cities, it could cause considerable and expensive damage and make storm surges more destructive as well.

## TAKE ACTION!

1. Become a climate ambassador. Information can be found here: http://www.epa.gov/climateforaction/lead/become.htm
2. Familiarize yourself with the International Youth Climate Movement and become active within this organization. If you are comfortable doing so, consider becoming involved locally by initiating an informal discussion group with friends.

## CHANGES TO FRESHWATER SYSTEMS

Global warming also affects surface water such as lakes and streams, in a similar way to the oceans. Not only would the water in the streams and rivers expand, but changing rainfall and snow patterns also affect the water level. More or less rain raises or lowers the levels of streams and lakes, as well as increasing or decreasing the usefulness of underground bodies of water called aquifers. Many people get their drinking water from such surface and subsurface water supplies, and if too little rain falls, those aquifers and rivers can run out of usable water, as we are seeing in California.

Although IPCC investigators reported unambiguous evidence that stream flows are changing, either over the course of the year or during peak periods of stream flow after major storms, this may be due to local weather effects.[5] While the levels of lakes and inland seas (such as the Caspian Sea) have varied over time, IPCC researchers point out that local weather effects can change the level of lakes and inland seas, which can perhaps mask or exaggerate global changes.

## LET IT SNOW

As we have explored in detail, climate change affects more than just the temperature. Because of its effects on things like cloudiness, humidity, and weather circulation patterns, a global temperature increase would also influence the rate of snowfall, the total snow depth that falls in a year, and the amount of the world covered by snow in any given year. Although studies examining changes in these snow characteristics show some ambiguity that is puzzling to scientists, widespread changes in snowfall levels are consistent with theories of climate destabilization. Snow cover (the total area covered by snow) has declined in recent years, with a higher percentage of moisture in cold areas coming down as rain, rather than snow. That is what one would expect if it really is warming up, as the temperature records discussed above suggest.

But while the area covered by snow in the Northern Hemisphere has declined by about 10 percent over the past thirty-six years, some areas have actually gotten more snowfall than usual. And while the extent of snow cover has fallen in the spring, it is increasing during winter, which is when the largest share of global warming is apparent.[6] Like the other climate trends discussed above, changes in snowfall are not spread evenly around the earth. Rather than decreasing, snow extent has increased in some parts of the world, even as the earth warms.[7] Observed changes in snowfall are not consistent in time, either. Snowfall over China decreased during the 1950s but increased during the 1960s and 1970s. Besides the area of the earth covered by snow in a given year, global warming changes

Scientists have found contradictory data on climate change and its effect on snow across the world. Some areas have seen a decrease in snowfall as temperatures increase, while others, puzzlingly, have had more snow than usual.

the average depth of snow. For example, snow-depth measurements in the former Soviet Union over the twentieth century show decreased snow depth of about 14 percent during the winter, mostly in the western portion of the ex-Union.

## ARCTIC TROUBLE

The earth has many masses of ice in cold areas, including glaciers, ice caps, ice sheets, and sea ice (such as icebergs). Climate investigators know that many of the world's glaciers have clearly shrunk over the last hundred years. But scientists' knowledge of when that shrinkage started and, therefore, its exact relationship to climate change is still evolving.[8]

Back in 2001, IPCC investigators identified some contradictory evidence of ice sheet change: While some evidence showed that the Greenland and Antarctic ice sheets were shrinking, other clues suggested they were actually growing. Still other evidence supported that some ice sheets, such as the Greenland ice sheet, may even be doing both, growing on top and shrinking at the edges.[9] Finally, regarding floating sea-ice masses such as icebergs, the evidence collected by climate investigators suggests that sea ice is covering a far smaller part of the Arctic Ocean during spring and summer months, compared to the historical average. In Antarctica, there is no clear trend in the coverage of the ocean by sea ice since 1973, when satellite measurements first began.[10] It soon became clear that more evidence would have to be gathered before changes in glaciers and ice sheets could be understood.

Now that we have more evidence, the picture emerging is that nowhere on Earth is climate change more visible and tangible than in the Arctic and Antarctic regions. Recent summers have been some of the warmest in four hundred years, and experts believe that the Arctic Ocean may have an ice-free summer by the middle of this century. While Arctic navigability is jubilant news to shipping and leisure cruising industries (ironically, both heavy polluters), it is entirely bad for almost everybody else. Because the landscapes of polar regions are determined in large part by the freezing point of water, warming increments that push beyond this point have a far greater effect in these areas than in tropical or subtropical regions. Moreover, cold, icy areas are far more susceptible to positive feedback loops that amplify change. For example, as ice disappears, more heat is absorbed into the dark-colored ocean, rather than bounced off the light reflective surface of ice. Finally, as temperatures warm, areas of permafrost will disappear. This is highly dangerous, as billions of tons of methane hydrates are trapped within this substance. Many researchers fear that the release of these compounds into the atmosphere could have runaway effects on global warming, raising the accepted degree thresholds of warming and threatening all life.

## TORNADOES AND OTHER STORMS

Finally, as with a pot of water on the stove, heating up the atmosphere would be expected to increase the severity and changeability of weather. Some researchers have looked for such evidence, after predicting that a warmer world would also have more frequent bouts of extreme weather, including hurricanes, tornadoes, dust storms, cyclones, and so on. Luckily, there is little evidence supporting these dire predictions on a global scale. IPCC climate investigators concluded in their 2001 Third Assessment Report that, "No systematic changes in the frequency of tornadoes, thunder days, or hail events are evident in the limited areas analysed."[11] Some of the changes have been toward more rapid changeability than usual, and some have been toward less rapid changeability.[12]

Two things are worth noting here. First, in the case of tornadoes, they can only occur under certain known and fixed meteorological conditions, many of which are determined by geography. Thus, it would be logical, and somewhat of a relief, to learn that climate change will not necessarily make their appearance more frequent or widespread, although it could slightly alter where they occur. Second, the IPCC stated that it has only used data from limited areas. Once data covering a greater area and timeframe are analyzed, these conclusions are liable to change as fast as the climate itself.

An increase in storms like Hurricane Katrina (viewed here by satellite) has not yet been seen, despite some predictions that climate change will cause more frequent severe weather.

## NOT OUT OF THE WOODS

Since the unusually hot summer of 1988, climate investigators have been on a quest to determine how rapidly the earth is heating up because of human action. To answer this question, researchers have gathered a massive amount of direct and circumstantial evidence, from thermometers, weather balloons, satellites, boreholes, ice cores, tree rings, rainfall readings, snowfall readings, icebergs, glaciers, and more.

Though climate investigators agree that the earth's surface is heating up at an alarming rate, its impacts on localized weather events are less clear. Trends in rainfall are mixed, as are trends in snowfall. Sea levels are clearly on the rise, but by precisely how much is not conclusive. Trends in the melting of glacial ice are in line with a continued warming of the earth since the last ice age, but even this trend is confusing, with some areas of the earth experiencing the growth of glaciers, even while the temperature is going up. Still, all climate investigators agree that the observed instabilities in these climate measurements are consistent with the earth warming up in unusual ways, and they identify the influence of humanity as the cause. Even with sometimes limited information, it would be a grave mistake to say, as some climate change skeptics have in the past, that those who are vigilant about climate justice suffer from an overly short-term point of view. In fact, quite the opposite is true.

This simple diagram illustrates how greenhouse gases contribute to the warming of the earth.

# CHAPTER 5

# DANGEROUS CARBON EMISSIONS

**HOW ARE RESEARCHERS SO CERTAIN HUMANS ARE** heating up the planet? If it is possible to find mixed circumstantial evidence of global warming based on weather effects, would this not cast doubt over the verdict that humanity is collectively responsible? Unfortunately, the answer here is no. While it is true that climate change is due to a complex array of factors, it is clear that human-made greenhouse emissions, or specifically, atmospheric carbon dioxide from the consumption of fossil fuels, are by far the leading contributor to our warming planet.

Before we illustrate how scientists have proved this, one has to understand the nature of the earth's atmosphere and the gases that make it up. The atmosphere is the layer of gases that surrounds the earth. The atmosphere is composed mostly of nitrogen and oxygen, but there are smaller quantities of other gases mixed in. Because most of these gases are transparent, we do not think about them very much, certainly not as something that affects the average temperature of the earth's surface.

However, as we discussed earlier, several of the gases in the earth's atmosphere—the greenhouse gases—play a key role in setting the thermostat of the earth's surface. The different gases found in the atmosphere, as Joseph Fourier showed, trap heat in different ways.

Scientists talk about the gases in the atmosphere using terms like parts per million and parts per billion. Sometimes they are talking about molecules, and sometimes they are talking about a certain volume of gas. For example, if there was one molecule of ozone in every million molecules found in a sample of the air, the concentration of ozone would be one part per million. If one gallon of ozone was found in every million gallons of air tested, the concentration would still be one part per million *by volume*, but because ozone molecules do not take up the same space that all the other gases do, there could be more or less than one molecule per million others in the sample. It is a hard thing to picture a million of anything, of course, and talking about the "space taken up" (or volume) of one invisible gas mixing with others is almost impossible to imagine. But scaling things down can help. Picture ninety-nine pennies lying on a desktop, with one dime mixed in among them. The "concentration" of dimes in that collection would be one dime per hundred. If you had a 999 pennies and one dime, it would be one dime per thousand, and so on. That is not too complicated.

It is a bit harder to imagine things by volume, but again, scaling things down should help. Imagine that you had ninety-nine cups of dimes on the table in front of you and one cup of quarters. If you were asked what the concentration of quarters was *in cups*, you would answer "one in one hundred." But if you were asked what the concentration of quarters was by number, you would realize that it is much less than one in one hundred, because many more dimes will fit into a cup than will quarters.

## WHAT IS CARBON DIOXIDE ($CO_2$)?

Carbon dioxide is a colorless and odorless gas. Each molecule of carbon dioxide is made up of one atom of carbon and two atoms of oxygen. Its chemical abbreviation, $CO_2$, reflects that proportion. Most of you know that carbon dioxide is the substance that plants take in from the air, converting it to sugar by tapping the power of sunlight, in the process called photosynthesis. That makes carbon dioxide essential for the growth of plants, trees, and crops. What you might not know is that carbon dioxide is also the gas that makes soda bubbly, as well as part of the gas that is released when you burn a piece of wood, coal, or gasoline.

Compared to nitrogen and oxygen, carbon dioxide accounts for a small percentage of the atmosphere, but that percentage is climbing fast. As of July 2015, 401.30 parts out of every million parts of the atmosphere are made up of carbon dioxide.[1] Despite what seems like a relative scarcity, researchers are very worried by the rapidly increasing percentage of atmospheric $CO_2$ and point out that the carbon dioxide level long considered safe is around 350 parts per million. Before the Industrial Revolution, when people started using large amounts of energy and causing significant changes to the environment by expanding farms and cities where forests used to be, carbon dioxide levels hovered near 280 parts per million, by volume. But even before humans were acting to change carbon dioxide levels, other forces did. Dips as low as 200 parts per million or surges into the mid-300 parts per million have been observed by climate investigators looking at air bubbles trapped in polar ice cores.

## THE CARBON CYCLE

The carbon in carbon dioxide is an element present in many forms of solid, liquid, and gaseous materials on earth. In fact, carbon moves through a cycle on the earth, spewing out into the atmosphere from the core of the earth when volcanoes erupt, then being trapped by land and water plants as sugar (sugar is made mostly of carbon). When combined with minerals, that sugar is used to make all the other chemicals in the bodies of plants and animals. After water, carbon makes up the largest part of your body, as it does for all animals and plants. The carbon bound up in living tissues is eventually returned to the carbon cycle after the animals and plants die. Through rainfall and the action of rivers and streams, carbon eventually washes out into the oceans and sinks to the bottom. In some areas of the ocean, and even some areas on land, a phenomenon called "plate tectonics" causes some of the earth's surface layers to slowly return to the core of the earth, and much of the carbon that plants and animals take out of the atmosphere is pulled back with it. Eventually, after the residual animal and plant materials are converted back to pure carbon, it is paired up with two molecules of oxygen, and carbon dioxide is spewed back out of volcanoes, starting the cycle all over again.

Starting with the Industrial Revolution, the carbon cycle has been significantly altered by humans, activity which is only accelerating when we need to be putting on the brakes. Carbon dioxide that is bound up in fossil fuels like coal and oil is released into the atmosphere much more quickly than it would through nonhuman processes. Human activities such as fuel burning and planting crops exert by far the biggest increase in the carbon dioxide concentration of the atmosphere, but ocean currents,

## GLOBAL CARBON CYCLE

Human activity has significantly affected the natural carbon cycle, depicted here, with the result being a much greater amount of carbon dioxide in the atmosphere.

volcanic eruptions, changes in atmospheric humidity, and other factors can exacerbate these changes.

Because carbon dioxide stays in the atmosphere for a long time and can be put into the air faster than it is taken out by plants or other processes, carbon dioxide has built up enormously in the atmosphere over time. The carbon dioxide humans release into the air stays there for about 120 years, and over many years, even a small contribution can add up to a big impact.[2] Other human actions besides fuel use (such as turning forested land into farmland or urban development) can also have a significant impact on the carbon cycle because of human impacts on the storage of carbon in vegetation and soil.

## MEASURING PAST LEVELS OF CARBON DIOXIDE

Evidence of carbon dioxide's atmospheric concentration in the past comes from indirect measurements, such as the analysis of gas bubbles trapped in Antarctic glaciers. Though this kind of indirect measurement is less accurate than directly measuring the carbon dioxide in the air, it is the only way we can determine what past levels of carbon dioxide were. That has helped scientists to understand how unusual the recent increases in carbon dioxide have been, from a historical point of view. But there are still many incompletely understood parts of the carbon cycle. Scientists are still unsure about why past increases in carbon dioxide levels sometimes occur before global warming, but sometimes comes after. They are also unsure of how much carbon dioxide the plants of the world can absorb, and for how long.

## THE KEELING CURVE

Highly accurate, direct measurement of carbon dioxide levels began in 1957, when Charles Keeling began collecting samples atop the Mauna Loa

Observatory in Hawaii. Within a few years, the data Keeling collected showed a steady increase in atmospheric carbon dioxide over the long term, and a distinctive "saw-tooth" patterned curve. The jagged curve Keeling observed was consistent with the seasons. In the fall and winter months in the large and wooded landmass of the Northern Hemisphere, elevated atmospheric levels of $CO_2$ could be expected. By converse, we would expect to see diminished levels with the greening of the land in the spring and summer, as plants act as a natural carbon sink. This is exactly what the data showed. Keeling's observations have been praised by James Hansen of NASA and others for clarity and accuracy. Since carbon dioxide distributes itself evenly in the air, readings based in the South Pacific are considered valid for the globe. Moreover, based on computer

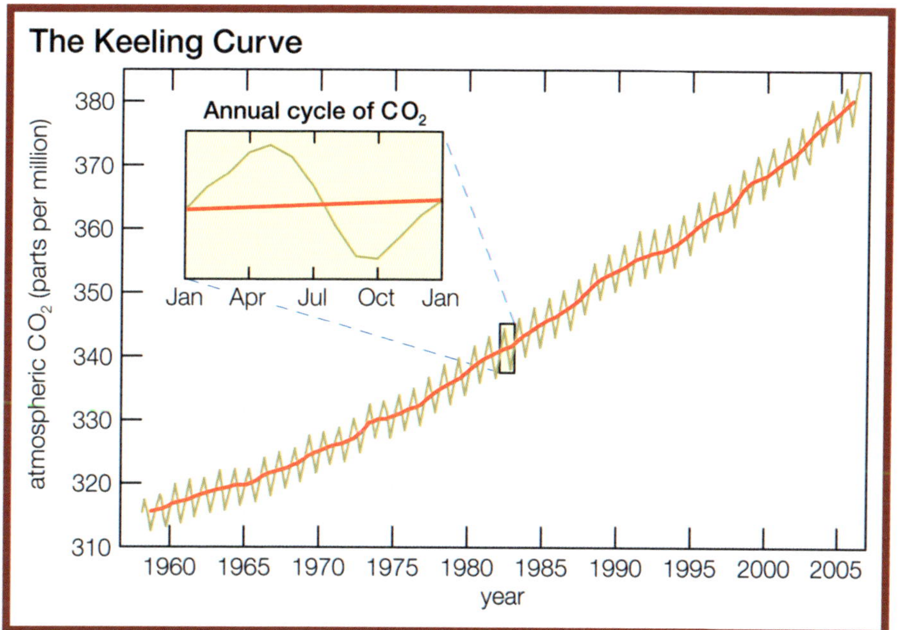


The Keeling curve tracks the long-term increase in the amount of carbon dioxide found in the atmosphere. The jagged pattern is a result of the fluctuations of the gas through the seasons.

analysis of the data, scientists are predicting that a doubling of the 1967 level of $CO_2$ could yield global temperature increases of about 3°C.

## METHANE

Methane is the second most prevalent and important greenhouse gas in the climate change picture. Like carbon dioxide, methane is a colorless, odorless gas. One molecule of methane consists of one atom of carbon and four atoms of hydrogen, giving it a chemical name of CH4. Methane is a major constituent of the natural gas that your stove, water heater, or other household devices use to heat water or to cook food.

Methane enters the atmosphere from a variety of sources, mostly of human origin, although some natural methane is emitted by natural sources. The natural gas, petroleum, and agricultural industries are all major producers of methane pollution. Furthermore, if the methane trapped in Arctic permafrost is released, this will be considered a human-caused source of methane, since warming would be the cause of its release. As a greenhouse gas, methane is a warming agent between five and fifty-six times more powerful than carbon dioxide, making it a true powerhouse of global warming, and as such, a growing concern to scientists if atmospheric concentrations are to quickly spike. The reason this warming strength has such a broad range is because the warming strength of all the different greenhouse gases is compared to carbon dioxide, which has a very long lifetime in the atmosphere. In other words, once carbon dioxide is put into the air, it takes a long time for it to be removed from the air by plants or other natural forces. Methane, on the other hand, has a much shorter lifetime in the atmosphere, only about twelve years. If one compares the warming ability of one gallon of carbon dioxide versus one gallon of methane over a five-year period, the methane's greater ability to trap heat will be obvious and give it a much higher heat-trapping ability. But if one looks over twenty years, the methane originally released will have been taken out of the atmosphere, while most of the carbon dioxide will still be there, trapping heat.

Methane is considered a trace gas, because it is found at low levels in the atmosphere—only 1.7 parts of methane are present in every million parts of air. But like carbon dioxide levels, methane levels have risen steadily in the last hundred years. Methane's concentration in the atmosphere has increased nearly 150 percent since the beginning of the nineteenth century, with current levels being the highest ever recorded. Despite its low concentrations, climate investigators have suggested that methane, more than carbon dioxide, has been the driving force behind

## TAKE ACTION!

1. Driving cars is a major source of carbon emissions. Are there ways you can cut down on your car use? Consider walking, using a bicycle, or taking public transportation whenever possible. If you must drive, look into purchasing a fuel-efficient or hybrid vehicle. Often, the savings in gasoline will more than offset the cost of upgrading to such a vehicle, and tax breaks are available for these cars as well.
2. Support local and national politicians who seek to increase clean and renewable energy production. These industries are important in paving the way forward and can also create jobs. If politicians oppose these industries, look into how their campaigns are funded.

rapid climate warming in the distant past.[3] More recently, James Hansen, the same investigator who galvanized action with his 1988 testimony to Congress, has suggested that although much attention must be paid to carbon dioxide as a warming gas, methane plays an important and underestimated role in recently observed global warming.[4]

## OTHER GREENHOUSE GASES

In 2013 nitrous oxide accounted for 5 percent of US greenhouse emissions.[5] Nitrous oxide is a colorless and almost odorless gas found in very low levels in the atmosphere. A molecule of nitrous oxide is made up of two atoms of nitrogen and one atom of oxygen. Nitrous oxide is also known by its nickname, "laughing gas," because it is sometimes used to make people feel relaxed and sleepy at the dentist's office, and, true to its name, it tends to make people a bit giggly. Nitrous oxide comes from a variety of sources, some of human origin such as agriculture and transportation and, others of natural origin.

Nitrous oxide is a long-lived warming gas with a relative warming strength up to nearly three hundred times that of carbon dioxide. Like methane, nitrous oxide has a shorter lifespan than carbon dioxide (114 years versus 120 for carbon dioxide). This means that nitrous oxide could have more or less global warming impact than carbon dioxide, depending on whether one is looking at shorter terms or longer terms. Like methane, nitrous oxide is considered a trace gas in the atmosphere, but at still lower levels, around 0.3 parts per million of the atmosphere by volume. Nitrous oxide concentrations have increased in recent years. Before the industrial age, concentrations of nitrous oxide hovered at an average of 279 parts per billion by volume.

Ozone is beneficial in the upper atmosphere, but when found lower to the earth's surface, it can be a pollutant in the form of smog.

Ozone, the slightly bluish, acrid-smelling gas composed of three atoms of oxygen bound together, is another compound considered to be a greenhouse gas. You may be familiar with the smell of ozone—it is the tangy smell sometimes given off by electronic devices like your television set. Ozone plays many different roles in the environment, depending on where it is found, and several of those roles are linked to each other.

At the very top of the atmosphere, in the stratosphere, ozone is a beneficial gas. Up there, ozone stops certain harmful rays of the sun (called ultraviolet, or UV, rays) from penetrating down to the surface of the earth, where they could harm plants or animals. That ozone layer forms right where it is, when high-energy radiation from the sun breaks apart normal oxygen (made of two atoms of oxygen bound together), and all the free oxygen atoms can combine into groups of three. You have probably heard that there is a "hole" in that beneficial ozone layer, and there is. The hole in the stratospheric ozone layer is partly a natural process due to the way air circulates around the earth and is partly a result of the actions of certain chemicals, called halocarbons. And this is where things get confusing. As will be discussed later, halocarbons are, themselves, global warming gases, but their effect on the stratospheric ozone layer is a separate process. Further complicating things, the ozone "hole" does change the way the earth's atmosphere retains heat. Finally, found down at ground level in a city, ozone is also called "smog" and can irritate people's eyes or the linings of their lungs.

Because of all those interactions, the impact of ozone on global warming can be downright confusing. At lower levels of the atmosphere (called the troposphere), scientists think that ozone exerts a warming force on the atmosphere. Tropospheric levels of ozone in the Northern Hemisphere may have doubled since the 1800s. But ozone concentrations in the Southern Hemisphere are uncertain, while at the Poles, tropospheric ozone concentrations seem to have fallen since the mid-1980s. At higher, or stratospheric, altitudes, ozone exerts a cooling force upon the atmosphere. Stratospheric ozone also shields the earth from some of the sun's more dangerous types of radiation, including ultraviolet radiation, the kind that causes sunburn and skin cancer. Ozone concentrations in the stratosphere have been declining over much of the earth, as much as 2 percent each decade for the last thirty years.[6] Much of the decline in stratospheric ozone concentrations has been attributed to the destructive action of halocarbons, discussed below.

## NON-GASEOUS ATMOSPHERIC SUBSTANCES

Aerosols are not gases but are liquid or solid particles small enough to stay suspended in the air, like fine mist. Both human and nonhuman processes generate aerosols. For example, when airplanes fly overhead, they leave a trail of aerosol droplets behind them, as the exhaust gases and unburned fuel go through chemical reactions with moisture in the air. When temperature and humidity conditions are right, this trail of aerosol droplets forms a brightly visible contrail behind the airplane.

Different aerosol types can have different impacts upon the climate. Some aerosol particles tend to absorb light and can exert a warming effect. Aerosols do not remain in the atmosphere for long periods of time, tending to be washed out of the air by rainfall on a regular basis. Interestingly, many aerosols that humans create are believed to have a cooling effect on the climate. On a global basis, scientists think that this cooling effect could cancel out some of the predicted warming from all the other greenhouse gases combined. But as with the observed warming, the cooling effects of aerosols are local and depend on local aerosol types and concentrations. The exact way that aerosols act as cooling agents is poorly understood. Besides directly scattering incoming sunlight, particulate matter can also increase the brightness, formation, and lifetime of clouds, affecting the reflection of incoming solar radiation back to space. While this may come as a bit of welcome good news, it is unlikely that aerosols can cancel out a significant enough portion of greenhouse gases to counter their warming effect.

The impact of aerosols on climate is a hotly debated issue among climate investigators. Some scientists argue that the cooling effects of aerosols have canceled out or hidden warming from other greenhouse

The trails left behind many jets may look like smoke, but these contrails are actually made of aerosol droplets formed from exhaust gases and unburned fuel.

gases. They say this will lead to more warming in the future, because different air pollution control laws are making aerosol concentrations decline. Other investigators argue that aerosols did not cause this kind of masking of global warming in the past. They observe that cooling and warming aerosols could cancel each other out altogether.

## HALOCARBONS

Halocarbons are human-made chemicals that are used as cooling agents and propellants in a broad range of devices such as air conditioners and refrigerators. In the past, halocarbons were also used as a gas for puffing up styrofoam and for cleaning off electrical circuit boards. There are many different types of halocarbons, some of which have been banned from production because of concerns about their adverse impacts upon the stratospheric ozone layer. Because of their destructive action on the stratospheric ozone layer, developed countries agreed not to produce certain halocarbons as part of an international accord called the Montreal Protocol. Other halocarbons that do not hurt the stratospheric ozone layer remain in production.

Halocarbons are thought to be very powerful warming gases. Some kinds are over ten thousand times more capable of trapping heat than is carbon dioxide. Halocarbons can also be very long-lived, persisting for many hundreds of years in the atmosphere after release. One group, called the perfluorocarbons, are virtually "immortal," persisting for up to fifty thousand years. Offsetting their greater heat-trapping ability is the fact that halocarbons are found at much lower concentrations than the other greenhouse gases. Whereas carbon dioxide is measured in parts per million, and methane in parts per billion, halocarbons are measured in parts per trillion.

Halocarbons can exert a variety of impacts on the climate, depending on the type of halocarbon involved and where it is found. Current scientific understanding of the global warming impact of halocarbons suggests that the ozone-depleting halocarbons (the production of which has been banned in many countries) exert a cooling effect. The newer halocarbons, those that do not destroy high-altitude ozone, seem to be pure warming gases but with a considerably lower warming potential than the chemicals they replaced. Because ozone chemistry in the atmosphere is so complex, scientists are uncertain about the ultimate impact of halocarbons on climate change.

Heavy, low clouds like these tend to have a cooling effect, while wispy cirrus clouds trap the sun's heat.

## CHAPTER 6

# EXTRA FACTORS IN THE MIX

**IN ADDITION TO THE LITANY OF GREENHOUSE GASES AND** other substances discussed in the previous chapter, climate investigators are faced with some additional causes of global warming that are not yet completely quantified and understood. While some of these factors may help cool the planet, most of these potential climate change factors are positive—that is, they could cause greater warming. Take for example water vapor, which we will discuss below. Water vapor's natural warming effects are amplified by a positive feedback loop: as more water vapor enters the atmosphere, higher temperatures cause more surface water to evaporate, perpetuating an ongoing cycle. However, the picture is somewhat complicated, as under certain conditions, water vapor acts as a cooling force as well.

## WATER, WATER, EVERYWHERE

Water vapor is by far the most abundant of the greenhouse gases and the dominant contributor to the natural greenhouse effect. On average, about 0.4 percent of all the molecules in the air are water molecules. That is about ten times as common as carbon dioxide. But the amount of water in the air varies by location. Some areas can have as much as 2 percent of the air filled with water vapor. Glaciers and ice caps contain about 1,900 times as much water as the total atmosphere does, while ground and surface waters hold about 660 times as much water as the total atmosphere does. The oceans hold over 100,000 times as much water as the entire earth's atmosphere.

Besides the total amount of water vapor in the atmosphere, climate investigators have to consider its distribution at different altitudes and locations, because small changes in water vapor can have significant local effects on climate. Almost all water vapor enters the atmosphere by evaporation, and about 90 percent of the earth's water vapor is in the half of the atmosphere closest to the earth's surface. At typical United States temperatures, perhaps 2 percent or more of the air molecules near the surface are water vapor, and this figure is increasing by as much as 1 percent per decade.

Water vapor plays a dual role in influencing the climate, functioning as either a climate-warming force or a climate-cooling force. When it enters the atmosphere via evaporation, water vapor cools the surface from which it evaporates and thus is a cooling force. The same thing happens to you when water evaporates from your skin—it cools you down. Another way that water vapor can cool the climate is when it takes the form of clouds that reflect incoming solar energy away from the earth. Low-level clouds are thicker and tend to cool the earth by reflecting energy away. By contrast, water vapor in the form of thin cirrus clouds acts as a warming force because it lets incoming energy pass through but stops some of the energy from bouncing back out into space. Water vapor also warms the climate by trapping heat even more effectively than carbon dioxide.

Most climate investigators think that a warmer world will lead to higher levels of water vapor and cause still more global warming. But a small minority thinks otherwise. Richard Lindzen, a respected climatologist at the Massachusetts Institute of Technology, points out that even if added evaporation due to global warming does occur, the higher energy levels predicted for storms at that temperature would force the vapor back out of the air more quickly, possibly canceling out the potential amplifying effect on warming. Further complicating the situation, climate investigators are not even sure if recently experienced warming has led to higher levels of water vapor in the air, as theories say it should.

Using satellites, some researchers have started gathering detailed information on water vapor levels in the atmosphere since the late 1970s. Some investigators have seen what appear to be slight increases in water vapor in various parts of the atmosphere, up to 13 percent. But other researchers, looking at the same information, have found just the opposite, pointing to an apparent drying of the atmosphere rather than increased moisture levels. Although we suspect that those predicting more water vapor are correct, what little information investigators do have suffers from the same kind of problems discussed for other climate information. Changes in measuring systems, changes in instrument type, limited geographic coverage, limited time span, and many other factors make information on water vapor too sketchy to allow for strong conclusions about how it has reacted to recent global warming or how it is likely to affect future global warming. Nonetheless, most climate researchers believe that water vapor is only a supporting player in the climate change drama and are far more concerned with carbon and other greenhouse emissions discussed in the previous chapter.

## GLOBAL DIMMING?

Given our reluctance to act quickly in the face of climate change, it is tempting to conclude that global dimming refers to diminishing levels of human intelligence around the globe. Rather, global dimming refers to a slight decrease in the percentage of sunlight reaching the earth's surface. This phenomenon, named by Gerald Stanhill, and prominently researched by Michael Roderick and Graham Farquhar, was identified in 2003 but began in the 1950s. According to two separate studies, global dimming yielded a drop in solar radiation somewhere between 1.3 and 2.7 percent per decade until the 1990s, when it appeared that the dimming reversed. This was due to the cleanup of aerosols and other light-blocking particles that caused the dimming. Thus, dimming could have been acting as an unseen cooling force while carbon emissions were on the rise. This is unfortunate news. If sunlight is now brightening, as some suspect, we have lost a cooling force at just the wrong time.

## SUN CYCLES

Rather than burning with a steady output, the sun burns hotter and cooler over time. Several cycles of increased or decreased solar output have been identified, including cycles at intervals of eleven years, twenty-two years, and eighty-eight years.

Highly accurate satellite measurements of the sun's output have only been taken since the early 1980s. But investigators can also learn about the sun's output from ice cores and tree rings. One way they can do this is by looking at the impact of cosmic rays (a type of radiation from the sun), which produce unique radioactive versions of certain elements. Beryllium is one such element; when it is hit by cosmic rays, some of it is changed into a slightly radioactive form that gets incorporated into trees as they grow or gets trapped in bubbles in ice masses, just as carbon dioxide does. Using this evidence, scientists have formed an idea of what the levels of solar energy reaching the earth have been. Taken as a whole, the evidence suggests that from AD 1600 to the present, the sun has clearly been running hotter, increasing the level of solar output, which constitutes the main natural influence on the temperature of the earth's climate system. Some investigators suggest that this increased solar energy level may have been responsible for half of the increase in temperature from 1900 through 1970 and for one third of the warming

Evidence shows that the sun is burning brighter now than it did several hundred years ago.

seen since 1970. Other climate investigators argue that the sun's output has not increased that much and think that it has not caused a significant share of the global warming observed since the 1970s.

## COUNTERING THE SKEPTICS

Even in the face of overwhelming evidence to the contrary, a very small but vocal contingent of climate investigators still think that the recently observed global warming is not of human origin at all but, rather, is part of the earth's natural cycle of climate change. Given that the IPCC and 97 percent of the scientific community are in total disagreement, how is this position defended? To briefly play devil's advocate, these researchers point to past periods in the planet's history, when average temperatures equaled or exceeded temperatures seen today. A long-standing assumption of nearly all climate investigators is that recently observed warming is abnormal and thus due to human activity. But skeptical researchers point to evidence that temperatures in the past have shown more rapid and extreme climate change than the recent changes seen globally. In Greenland, temperatures increased in the past by as much as 7°C over only a few decades. Sea-surface temperatures in the Norwegian Sea also changed rapidly in the past, warming by as much as 5°C in less than forty years.[1] Recently, some climate investigators have suggested that these temperature fluctuations were not only local in scale but were actually global. If past global average temperatures exceeded those of today, these investigators argue, it is possible that we are simply experiencing a normal fluctuation, and while human activity may be slightly accentuating that fluctuation, it is not the cause.

Putting aside for a moment the cynical notion that these skeptics are in partnership with the well-funded fossil-fuel industry and their associated

## TAKE ACTION!

1. Find ways to save energy at home. Turn off all electrical devices and lights whenever possible. Switch to energy efficient compact fluorescent bulbs, use a low-flow shower nozzle, and use climate-friendly fuels such as wood or passive solar glass to offset the amount of heating oil required in the winter.
2. Read up on permaculture and radically sustainable building practices. Even if you do not have the ability to build a cob or strawbale house with your own two hands (very few of us do), the insights and experiences of those who have taken this path in their domestic lives provides many valuable and fascinating perspectives.

PR firms and lobbyists, mainstream climatologists have already rebutted the argument that natural variation is the primary driver of global temperature increases on the grounds of poor science. For example, a leading 2003 paper by Willie Soon and Sallie Baliunas arguing this position in the scientific journal *Climate Research* prompted even the journal's own publisher to acknowledge that it should have "insisted on solid evidence and more careful formulations" before publication. Moreover, even if some natural variation is adding to climate change, this does not negate the centuries of solid science and physical evidence upon which the theory of greenhouse warming is based. Finally, even if climate change were natural, what are the implications of taking this unlikely position? Would it enable the moral imperatives of climate justice, or would it further entrench corporate interests and status-quo politics?

# CHAPTER 7

# COMPUTING THE CHANGES

**THE USE OF COMPUTERS TO PREDICT THE WEATHER** has been an important application of computer science ever since the field exploded in the post-war years. When discussing computer modeling, it is important to reiterate the difference between weather and climate. Computers have been successfully employed for short-term weather predictions for decades. With fewer numbers and variables to crunch, this has been a complicated but nonetheless possible operation. On the other hand, climate modeling is dizzyingly complex, comprising many interdependent variables.

Computer models assign mathematical equations to things that happen in the real world. In climate models, investigators assign equations to things such as the incoming heat from the sun, the outgoing heat from the clouds or surface, the heat moved around in the ocean, the heat moved around in the air, and so on. Then they link all those equations together, and they do experiments with this model to see what might happen if they varied one part or another.

Computer models have been used to ask three main questions in global warming research. The first question is, "Is the climate changing abnormally?" This is sometimes called the detection of climate change. The second question that computer models are used to explore is, "What is causing the climate change we have observed?" This is sometimes called

Investigators use computer models of earth, like this one, to test theories of global warming.

the attribution of climate change. Finally, computer models are used to explore the question, "What would happen if the earth got warmer?" This is sometimes called the impact of climate change. The models can show how changes in the climate might affect humans, plants, and society. Answering each of these questions involves using different types of models that reflect different elements of climate science.

In trying to detect whether the climate is changing abnormally, investigators are trying to find out whether the warming that has been observed is greater than random chance. Computer models have been run with all of the evidence discussed previously and more as well, looking back over a thousand years to determine whether or not recent changes in the climate are from natural variation or not. With the power of new computer models, IPCC investigators are increasingly convinced that "most of the observed warming over the last fifty years is likely to have been due to the increase in greenhouse gas concentrations."[1] In looking for the cause of climate change, climate investigators for the IPCC and elsewhere are also increasingly confident that Arrhenius, Fourier, and Hansen were right—greenhouse gases are heating up the earth, at least over the last fifty years.

But when it comes to making predictions of the future, climate investigators might as well consult a fortune-teller. Computer models used to make predictions of the future are much less advanced than those used to detect global warming or to examine potential causes. While some investigators in the IPCC place confidence in long-term and regional predictions of increased temperature, sea level, rainfall, and so on, others are much less sure about predictive climate models.

Still, computer models are the only tools that climate investigators have to ask the most important questions about climate change. Is the climate changing abnormally? If so, what is behind the change, and what will the future look like? Computer models strongly suggest that it has warmed up, and warming has been caused by human emission of greenhouse gases. More specific and precise answers as to which human activities are causing the majority of the recent warming, and what things might look like in a warmer world, will take some years to find, while climate investigators continue to dig for more information.

## TAKE ACTION!

1. ClimatePrediction.net is a climate simulation web network that derives its processing power from an aggregate of individual PC users. By downloading the software, you can take part in this fascinating public undertaking to model climate change with computers. Although a few outlier results predict a greater temperature increase than what most scientists believe is coming, much of the site's data are in line with average predictions.
2. Take a look at the website co2now.org to learn more about rising levels of carbon dioxide in the atmosphere.

In 2014 citizens from around the world participated in the People's Climate March to raise awareness of this critical issue.

## CHAPTER 8

# HOPE DEPENDS ON ACTION

**MORE THAN A QUARTER-CENTURY HAS PASSED SINCE** the broiling, game-changing summer of 1988, the global warming equivalent of a three-alarm fire. Beginning with the 1992 Earth Summit in Rio de Janeiro and the Kyoto Protocol of 1997, the world community took important early steps to acknowledge and deal with the problem of human-caused, also known as anthropogenic, climate change. But these slow, incremental, and, in some cases, non-binding measures have not done enough to arrest the greenhouse emissions driving climate change. As a result, we have entered a pivotal moment: Computer models suggest that we will lock in extremely dangerous temperature increases, triggering a chain reaction of chaotic effects incompatible with a civilized world order—simply by continuing on our current emission trajectory. In other words, it is no longer sufficient to merely stabilize carbon emissions. If we are to have a 60 percent chance of staying within the 2°C global temperature increase thought to be safe, we must sharply and immediately cut greenhouse emissions by 15 to 30 percent below their levels in the 1990s. This daunting goal is only possible if we harness every available political and technological tool to reduce emissions and sequester atmospheric greenhouse gases. Unfortunately, powerful forces stand in the way.

On the other side of the coin, multi-national energy corporations are more determined than ever to increase production, ignoring all evidence that this business model is harmful, even fatal, to the planet. The profitability of these firms is dependent on removing carbon-based fossil fuels and methane gas from the ground and supplying it to the marketplace. This requires still more carbon-intensive shipping to developing economies in Asia. As conventional oil reserves are depleted, novel methods of extraction are being devised. Naomi Klein refers to this as "extreme extraction" and includes within the category controversial, highly risky practices such as hydraulic fracturing, better known as "fracking," mountaintop coal removal, deepwater and Arctic oil drilling, and the removal of bituminous coal from remote locations such as Canada's Alberta Tar Sands. Because of these messy, accident-prone, and occasionally deadly practices, Klein and others suggest that energy companies are now rogue actors in the economy and should be delegitimized just as tobacco companies have recently been.

The good news is that a broad coalition of leaders and ordinary people around the world are actively doing just that, deploying successful strategies such as blockades and invocations of indigenous peoples' rights to stop or delay new extraction projects. These bright spots have supplied much-needed hope to the climate justice movement. But we need all these victories and more, plus a serious commitment to clean energy such as wind and solar, if we are to reduce emissions to acceptable levels—levels that do not even guarantee a stable future climate.

## RIO DE JANEIRO, KYOTO, AND EXETER

The primary legacy of the Rio de Janeiro Earth Summit was an agreement called the UN Framework Convention on Climate Change. Although the UNFCC was vague on deadlines and targets, it stated that "lack of absolute scientific certainty" should not stand in the way of action where "threats of serious or irreversible damage" exist, a cautious and altogether rational claim that skeptics have nonetheless disregarded ever since. Moreover, the agreement highlighted the idea that the burden of relieving climate change falls unequally on nations, according to their different development histories. Finally, the accord argued for transparency with regard to yearly levels of greenhouse emissions. It would take until the Kyoto Protocol of 1997 for any actual emission reduction guidelines to be set. Because these targets varied between nations, Kyoto has been fraught with political and logistical problems and struggles. Neither the United States nor Australia ratified the treaty, so it took until 2004 when Russia ratified for Kyoto to become international law in 2005. In the meantime, many valuable years of emission reduction were lost, precisely when we could not afford the luxury of delay.

In 2005 a conference convened in Exeter, England, to determine how much global warming the globe could withstand before truly destructive consequences set in. Researchers in Exeter agreed that the 2°C mark is the upper limit of acceptable warming. They found that a 3°C warmer world could cause ice sheets in Greenland and the Antarctic to melt. This would change carbon sinks into carbon sources, potentially creating runaway effects. They also found that a 2°C world is rapidly slipping out of reach, as this target would have required major emission reductions by 2012. Discouragingly, emissions in the United States have actually gone up

Forests play a crucial role in reducing the amount of carbon dioxide in our atmosphere. Planting more trees (rather than cutting them down) can be an important step in reducing climate change.

since then and show no sign of slowing down. This is a serious cause for alarm for all who are paying attention.

## CUTTING DOWN ON CARBON

Reducing the emission of greenhouse gases is the most essential step to addressing global warming. However, many experts suggest we might also simultaneously explore actions that pull carbon dioxide, the main greenhouse gas, back out of the air. As we know, plants naturally pull carbon dioxide out of the air. Once locked up in solid form in trees, plants, and in woody material in the soil, carbon dioxide is less threatening to the climate.

There are three major ways people propose to hold carbon dioxide in solid form and reduce its global warming impacts. The first way involves forests. Sometimes, in different parts of the world, when trees are cut down for use as fuel, or for the paper or lumber industries, the area where the trees were is not replanted, or the land is put to non-forestry or non-farming uses. Climate investigators looking for ways to pull carbon dioxide out of the air point out that this practice limits the earth's natural ability to regulate greenhouse gases, including carbon dioxide. Preventing this kind of long-term removal of plants or crops from areas that have had trees removed can increase the amount of carbon dioxide pulled out of the air. Another approach to pulling carbon dioxide out of the air is to plant more trees, something almost everyone can support. Not only could more trees be planted in tree farms but tree-planting can be increased in cities and on land that is no longer good for growing crops.

Besides using trees to remove carbon dioxide from the air, some researchers think significant amounts of carbon dioxide could be stored in farm soils. They point out that some farming practices keep carbon dioxide locked away in the soil, rather than putting it back into the air where it harms the climate. Tilling the soil (digging it up prior to planting crops) is one farming practice that puts carbon dioxide back into the air but is not always necessary for crop cultivation. Also, changing the way that fertilizers and weed killers are used can help keep more carbon-bearing matter underground and prevent it from being broken down by microbes living in the soil. Finally, farm fields that are left

**TAKE ACTION!**

Up until this point, *Take Action* has focused on what you can do as an individual and with good reason. This is the only place to start. But there are limits to thinking and acting as an individual, especially with a problem as large and all-encompassing as climate change. Pick one issue that relates to climate change in your local area, and explore the ways it links to issues others are experiencing nationally or globally. How might such common ground help strengthen disparate threads of the climate justice and environmental movements?

bare after harvest are more likely to release their soil carbon back into the atmosphere. Planting cover crops, such as beans, on areas that are not being used for other food crops can preserve soil nutrients and keep carbon dioxide locked up in the soil.[1]

Carbon capture and storage (CCS) is an idea that has gained some traction following a 2005 IPCC special report on the subject. If engineers devise reliable ways to capture carbon gas released at the source of pollution before it enters the atmosphere, they could store this carbon in locations underground such as depleted wells. CCS is being attempted in limited ways, mostly in Europe, but the idea has attracted some criticism for failing to tackle the emissions problem from the root. Nonetheless, it is another tool that could help keep unwanted carbon out of the atmosphere while clean energy options are developed and implemented.

## CLEAN ENERGY

Common forms of renewable energy include wind, solar, hydro, and geothermal. Our search for cleaner energy is often framed as a technological problem, and while it is true that renewables have some technical hurdles to overcome, the fact is that most of these sources are long-running and proven technologies. Solar energy has been used extensively since the 1970s and is currently growing by 30 percent per year. Similar growth figures have been reported for wind energy. So why have these technologies failed to catch on in a way that significantly reduces our dependency on fossil fuels? Reliability is a concern, as is delay time in getting energy to the grid, particularly with the case of wind. However, lack of political

Wind and solar energy are two examples of effective renewable resources that reduce the amount of fossil fuels burned.

will and investment is by far the greatest roadblock to widespread use of renewables. Again, one might point a finger at the fossil fuel industry. With deep pockets, these companies actively lobby support away from renewable energy to keep profits high.

## A NEW MODEL FOR CLIMATE ACTION

While the above picture may appear grim indeed, we urge readers to channel anger and frustration into intelligent and caring action, rather than apathy and despair. Again, Naomi Klein's study is instructive: She identifies climate change as a galvanizing issue, drawing together many unlikely allies in the struggle for a more inhabitable planet, now and into the future. Railing against "Big Green" (environmental groups who pay lip service to climate justice while accepting money from its foes) and a top-down model of environmentalism, Klein identifies countless examples of people who do not fit the stereotypical profile of "activists" who are getting involved in their local communities to affect climate change in a positive direction.

# APPENDIX

**EXCERPTS FROM "CLIMATE CHANGE 2014, SYNTHESIS** Report," Intergovernmental Panel on Climate Change:

## OBSERVED CHANGES IN THE CLIMATE SYSTEM

Each of the last three decades has been successively warmer at the Earth's surface than any preceding decade since 1850. The period from 1983 to 2012 was likely the warmest 30-year period of the last 1400 years in the Northern Hemisphere, where such assessment is possible (medium confidence). The globally averaged combined land and ocean surface temperature data as calculated by a linear trend show a warming of 0.85 [0.65 to 1.06] °C[2] over the period 1880 to 2012, when multiple independently produced datasets exist.

In addition to robust multi-decadal warming, the globally averaged surface temperature exhibits substantial decadal and interannual variability. Due to this natural variability, trends based on short records are very sensitive to the beginning and end dates and do not in general reflect long-term climate trends. As one example, the rate of warming over the past 15 years (1998–2012; 0.05 [–0.05 to 0.15] °C per decade), which begins with a strong El Niño, is smaller than the rate calculated since 1951 (1951–2012; 0.12 [0.08 to 0.14] °C per decade).

Ocean warming dominates the increase in energy stored in the climate system, accounting for more than 90 percent of the energy accumulated between 1971 and 2010 (high confidence), with only about 1 percent stored in the atmosphere. On a global scale, the ocean warming is largest near the surface, and the upper 75 m warmed by 0.11 [0.09 to 0.13] °C per decade over the period 1971 to 2010. It is virtually certain that the upper ocean (0–700 m) warmed from 1971 to 2010, and it likely warmed between the 1870s and 1971.

Averaged over the mid-latitude land areas of the Northern Hemisphere, precipitation has increased since 1901 (medium confidence before and high confidence after 1951). For other latitudes, area-averaged long-term positive or negative trends have low confidence. Observations of changes in ocean surface salinity also provide indirect evidence for changes in the global water cycle over the ocean (medium confidence). It is very likely that regions of high salinity, where evaporation dominates, have become more saline, while regions of low salinity, where precipitation dominates, have become fresher since the 1950s.

Since the beginning of the industrial era, oceanic uptake of $CO_2$ has resulted in acidification of the ocean; the pH of ocean surface water has decreased by 0.1 (high confidence), corresponding to a 26 percent increase in acidity, measured as hydrogen ion concentration.

Over the period 1992 to 2011, the Greenland and Antarctic ice sheets have been losing mass (high confidence), likely at a larger rate over 2002 to 2011. Glaciers have continued to shrink almost worldwide (high confidence). Northern Hemisphere spring snow cover has continued to decrease in extent (high confidence). There is high confidence that permafrost temperatures have increased in most regions since the early 1980s in response to increased surface temperature and changing snow cover.

The annual mean Arctic sea-ice extent decreased over the period 1979 to 2012, with a rate that was very likely in the range 3.5 to 4.1 percent per decade. Arctic sea-ice extent has decreased in every season and in every successive decade since 1979, with the most rapid decrease in decadal mean extent in summer (high confidence). It is very likely that the annual mean Antarctic sea-ice extent increased in the range of 1.2 to 1.8 percent per decade between 1979 and 2012. However, there is high confidence that there are strong regional differences in Antarctica, with extent increasing in some regions and decreasing in others.

Over the period 1901 to 2010, global mean sea level rose by 0.19 [0.17 to 0.21] m. The rate of sea level rise since the mid-19th century has been larger than the mean rate during the previous two millennia (high confidence).

## IMPACTS OF CLIMATE CHANGE

Evidence of observed climate change impacts is strongest and most comprehensive for natural systems. In many regions, changing precipitation or melting snow and ice are altering hydrological systems, affecting water resources in terms of quantity and quality (medium confidence). Many terrestrial, freshwater and marine species have shifted their geographic ranges, seasonal activities, migration patterns, abundances and species interactions in response to ongoing climate change (high confidence). Some impacts on human systems have also been attributed to climate change, with a major or minor contribution of climate change distinguishable from other influences. Assessment of many studies covering a wide range of regions and crops shows that negative impacts of climate change on crop yields have been more common than positive impacts (high confidence). Some impacts of ocean acidification on marine organisms have been attributed to human influence (medium confidence).

## EXTREME EVENTS

It is very likely that the number of cold days and nights has decreased and the number of warm days and nights has increased on the global scale. It is likely that the frequency of heat waves has increased in large parts of Europe, Asia and Australia. It is very likely that human influence has contributed to the observed global scale changes in the frequency and intensity of daily temperature extremes since the mid-20th century. It is likely that human influence has more than doubled the probability of occurrence of heat waves in some locations. There is medium confidence that the observed warming has increased heat-related human mortality and decreased cold-related human mortality in some regions.

There are likely more land regions where the number of heavy precipitation events has increased than where it has decreased. Recent detection of increasing trends in extreme precipitation and discharge in some catchments implies greater risks of flooding at regional scale (medium confidence). It is likely that extreme sea levels (for example, as experienced in storm surges) have increased since 1970, being mainly a result of rising mean sea level.

Impacts from recent climate-related extremes, such as heat waves, droughts, floods, cyclones and wildfires, reveal significant vulnerability and exposure of some ecosystems and many human systems to current climate variability (very high confidence).

*To view the report in its entirety, go to:*
https://www.ipcc.ch/report/ar5/syr/

# CHAPTER NOTES

## Chapter 1. Climate Change: A Most Urgent Matter

1. "Statement on Climate Change From 18 Scientific Associations," 2009, http://www.aaas.org/sites/default/files/migrate/uploads/1021climate_letter1.pdf.

2. Blue Planet Laureates, "Environmental and Development Challenges: The Imperative to Act," 2012, http://www.af-info.or.jp/en/bpplaureates/.

3. Robert Henson, *The Rough Guide to Climate Change* (New York: Penguin Putnam, 2006), 199.

4. "Statement of Dierdre A. Lee, Acting Deputy Director for Management, Office of Management and Budget Before the U.S. House of Representatives Subcommittee on National Economic Growth, Natural Resources, and Regulatory Affairs Committee on Government Reform and Oversight, and the United States Senate Subcommittee on Energy Research, Development, Production and Regulation, Committee on Energy and Natural Resources," May 20, 1999, http://www.whitehouse.gov/ omb/legislative/testimony/test052099ddm.html.

5. James West, "1988 Midwest Drought," *USA Today*, November 21, 1999, http://www.usatoday .com/2000/century/weather/stories/w88drought.htm.

6. Gale E. Christianson, *Greenhouse: The 200-Year Story of Global Warming* (New York: Walker and Company, 1999), p. 197.

7. West.

8. Michigan Department of State Police, "Extreme Temperatures," http://www.msp .state.mi.us/division/emd/Hazann2000/4-temperatures_MIHAZAN5.pdf (accessed Dec. 7, 2001).

9. Kevin Sanders, "Yellowstone National Parks Year of Fire: The Great Fires of 1988," 1996, http://www.yellowstone-bearman.com/bearman/ yfire.html.

10. G. Jendritsky, WOM/UNESCO Sub-Forum on Science and Technology: Extreme Temperatures, Presentation, http://www.unisdr.org/unisdr/ forum/tempwmo.htm (accessed Dec. 10, 2001).

11. James Hansen, "Testimony before the Committee on Energy and Commerce, United States House of Representatives," July 7, 1988.

12. Intergovernmental Panel on Climate Change (IPCC), *Climate Change 2001: The Scientific Basis* (Cambridge, MA: Cambridge University Press, 2001).

## Chapter 2. The Theory and Reality of Global Climate Change

1. N. Murray and M. Holman, "The Role of Chaotic Resonances in the Solar System," *Nature* 410 (April 12, 2001): 773–779.

2. James Rodger Fleming, *Historical Perspectives on Climate Change* (New York: Oxford University Press, 1998), 58.

3. Adapted from A. Bernarde, *Global Warning ... Global Warming* (New York: John Wiley & Sons, 1992), 26.

4. James Rodger Fleming, *Historical Perspectives on Climate Change* (New York: Oxford University Press, 1998), 58.

5. Ibid.

6. Ibid.

7. Barbara J. Finlayson-Pitts and James N. Pitts, Jr., *Chemistry of the Upper and Lower Atmosphere* (New York: Academic Press, 2000), 762.

8. Robert Henson, *The Rough Guide to Climate Change* (New York: Penguin Putnam, 2006), 28.

9. World Bank Group, *Turn Down the Heat: Confronting the New Climate Normal*, (Washington, DC: World Bank, 2014), https://openknowledge.worldbank.org/handle/10986/20595.

10. Naomi Klein, *This Changes Everything, Capitalism vs. The Climate* (New York: Simon and Schuster, 2015), 13.

11. Henson, 105.

12. Jonathan Topaz, "Jerry Brown: Fires Related to Climate Change," *Politico.com*, May 18, 2014, http://www.politico.com/blogs/politico-now/2014/05/jerry-brown-fires-related-to-climate-change-188729.

13. "Drought and climate change fuel high-elevation California fires, study finds," *Phys.org*, July 27, 2015, http://phys.org/news/2015-07-drought-climate-fuel-high-elevation-california.html

14. Fleming, 58.

15. Richard Stone, "If the Mercury Soars, So May Health Hazards," News and Comment, *Science* 267 (February 17, 1995): 957–958; Rita R. Colwell, "Global Climate and Infectious Disease: The Cholera Paradigm," Association Affairs, *Science* 274 (December 20, 1996): 2025–2031; Gary Taubes, "Apocalypse Not," News and Comment, *Science* 278 (November 7, 1997): 1004–1006.

## Chapter 3. Gathering Evidence of a Warming Planet

1. The largest collection of surface temperature data is maintained by the United States National Oceanographic and Atmospheric Association, www.noaa.gov.

2. Adapted from D. E. Parker, P. D. Jones, A. Bevan and C. K. Folland, "Interdecadal changes of surface temperature since the late 19th century," *Journal of Geophysical Research* 99 (1994): 14373–14399 (and updates).

3. Patrick J. Michaels and Robert C. Balling Jr., *The Satanic Gases: Clearing the Air About Global Warming* (Washington, DC: Cato Institute, 2000), 75–91.

4. Kenneth Green, *Exploring the Science of Climate Change* (Los Angeles: Reason Public Policy Institute, 1997), 19.

5. James Rodger Fleming, *Historical Perspectives on Climate Change* (New York: Oxford University Press, 1998), 17–18; Michael L. Parsons, *Global Warming, the Truth Behind the Myth* (New York: Plenum Press, 1995), 127.

6. Adapted from Parker, Jones, Bevan, and Folland.

7. J. R. Christy, R. W. Spencer, and W. D. Brasell, "MSU Tropospheric temperatures: Data set construction and radiosonde comparisons," *Journal of Atmospheric and Oceanic Technology* 17 (2000), 1153–1170 (and updates).

8. J. K. Angell, "Variations and trends in tropospheric and stratospheric global temperature, 19582/8/0287," *Journal of Climate* 1 (1988): 1296–1313 (and updates).

9. John Christy, written testimony before the United States Senate Committee on Environment and Public Works, May 2, 2001.

10. National Research Council, *Reconciling Observations of Global Temperature Change* (Washington, DC: National Academy Press, 2000), 2.

11. J. R. Petit et al., "Climate and atmospheric history of the past 420,000 years from the Vostok ice core, Antarctica," *Nature* 393 (June 3, 1999): 429–436.

12. Paleoclimatology Program, United States National Oceanographic and Aeronautic Administration (NOAA), accessed December 7, 2001, http://www.ngdc.noaa. gov/paleo/borehole/core.html.

13. J. Jouzel et al., "Validity of the temperature reconstruction from water isotopes in ice cores," *Journal of Geophysical Research* 102, no. C12 (November 30, 1997): 471–487.

14. Edward R. Cook, "Temperature Histories from Tree Rings and Corals," *Climate Dynamics* 11 (1995): 211–222.

## Chapter 4. Hazardous Effects of Climate Change

1. Intergovernmental Panel on Climate Change (IPCC), *Climate Change 1995: The Science of Climate Change* (Cambridge, MA: Cambridge University Press, 1996), 142.

2. Intergovernmental Panel on Climate Change (IPCC), *Climate Change 2001: The Scientific Basis* (Cambridge, MA: Cambridge University Press, 2001), 641.

3. Ibid., 666.

4. Ibid., 641.

5. Intergovernmental Panel on Climate Change (IPCC), *Climate Change 1995: The Science of Climate Change*, 158.

6. Intergovernmental Panel on Climate Change (IPCC), *Climate Change 2001: The Scientific Basis*, 123.

7. Ibid., 124.

8. Ibid., 129.

9. Intergovernmental Panel on Climate Change (IPCC), *Climate Change 1995: The Science of Climate Change*, 650–654.

10. Intergovernmental Panel on Climate Change (IPCC), *Climate Change 2001: The Scientific Basis*, 30.

11. Ibid., 5.

12. Intergovernmental Panel on Climate Change (IPCC), *Climate Change 1995: The Science of Climate Change*, 173.

## Chapter 5. Dangerous Carbon Emissions

1. "Earth's $CO_2$ Home Page," *$CO_2$Now.org*, http://co2now.org/.

2. For an up-to-date listing of the concentrations, lifetimes, and global warming ability of the different greenhouse gases, visit the Carbon Dioxide Information Analysis Center, hosted by the Oak Ridge National Laboratories, http://cdiac.ornl.gov/.

3. Richard A. Kerr, "A smoking gun for an ancient methane discharge," *Science* 286 (November 19, 1999): 1465.

4. James Hansen et al., "Climate Forcings in the Industrial Era," *Proceedings of the National Academy of Sciences* 95 (October 1998): 12753–12758.

5. Environmental Protection Agency, "Overview of Greenhouse Gases," *EPA.gov*, http://epa.gov/climatechange/ghgemissions/gases/n2o.html.

6. Intergovernmental Panel on Climate Change (IPCC), *Climate Change 2001: The Scientific Basis* (Cambridge, MA: Cambridge University Press, 2001), 256.

## Chapter 6. Extra Factors in the Mix

1. M. E. Raymo et al., "Millennial-scale climate instability during the early Pleistocene epoch," *Nature* 392 (April 16, 1998): 669–702.

## Chapter 7. Computing the Changes

1. Intergovernmental Panel on Climate Change (IPCC), *Climate Change 2001: The Scientific Basis* (Cambridge, MA: Cambridge University Press, 2001), 10.

# GLOSSARY

**aerosol**—Microscopic droplets of water and other chemicals that can either trap heat like a greenhouse gas or reflect heat away from the earth.

**afforestation**—Planting of new forests on lands that have not recently been forested.

**anthropogenic**—Relating to or denoting the current geological age, viewed as the period during which human activity is the dominant influence on climate and the environment.

**atmosphere**—The layer of gases that surrounds a planet.

**carbon dioxide**—A greenhouse gas consisting of one atom of carbon and two of oxygen, abbreviated $CO_2$.

**chaos**—The tendency of complex systems to vary randomly over time.

**climate**—The long-term (thirty-year) average pattern of the weather.

**ecosystem**—An assembly of plants, animals, insects, and other living things that constitutes a defined ecological system. Examples include forests, deserts, and wetlands.

**evaporation**—When water passes from a liquid into a vapor.

**fossil fuels**—Fuels derived from the tissues of living things from long ago. Fossil fuels include coal, peat, oil, and natural gas.

**global warming**—Warming of the earth's surface through the heat-trapping effects of certain greenhouse gases in the atmosphere.

**greenhouse effect**—The trapping of heat by certain greenhouse gases in the atmosphere.

**greenhouse gas**—Any gas that can trap heat in a planet's atmosphere that would otherwise pass back out into space.

**halocarbons**—Chemicals used in refrigerators and air conditioners. Halocarbons are strong greenhouse gases but are found at very low concentrations in the atmosphere.

**invertebrates**—Animals without a backbone, such as insects, octopuses, snails, and clams.

**latitude**—A measure of distance north or south of the earth's equator.

**longitude**—A measure of distance east or west from an imaginary line running from the North to South Poles, passing through the city of Greenwich, England.

**methane**—A greenhouse gas consisting of one atom of carbon and four of hydrogen, abbreviated CH4.

**nitrous oxide**—A greenhouse gas consisting of one atom of nitrogen and two atoms of oxygen. Also known as laughing gas.

**ozone**—A greenhouse gas consisting of three atoms of oxygen. Ozone plays many roles in the environment and is found at different levels of the atmosphere. In some cases, ozone can be protective; in other cases, it can cause harm to human, plant, and animal health directly.

**rain gauge**—A device for measuring rainfall.

**reforestation**—Replanting of forests on lands that have recently been harvested.

**renewable energy**—Energy obtained from sources such as geothermal, wind, photovoltaic, solar, and biomass.

**smog**—Another name for ozone when it is close to the ground, where people can inhale it.

**soot**—Fine particles of matter created through the combustion of fuel or mechanical friction.

**stratosphere**—The part of the atmosphere above the troposphere, extending about twenty miles above the earth's surface.

**thermostat**—A device that controls heating and cooling systems to maintain a specified temperature in an enclosed space, such as a room or refrigerator.

**troposphere**—The lower part of the atmosphere, from ground level up, ranging from four to eleven miles above the ground depending on where one is located on the earth's surface.

**Tyndall Effect**—The scattering of light by dust and large molecules. This is the effect that makes the sky look blue. Named for the discoverer, John Tyndall.

**wetlands**—Areas where there is a frequent and prolonged presence of water at or near the soil surface. Swamps, marshes, and bogs are examples of wetlands.

# FOR MORE INFORMATION

### Youth for Environmental Sanity (YES!)

www.yesworld.org/

Connects and inspires young changemakers to join forces to find sustainable ways of life.

### 350.org

350.org/

A global climate movement including online campaigns, grassroots organizing, and mass public actions.

### Student Environmental Youth Action Coalition

www.seac.org/

A network whose mission it is to share stories, skills, and knowledge to create sustainable communities.

### SustainUS

sustainus.org/

Dedicated to empowering young people to advance sustainable development.

### TakingITGlobal

issues.tigweb.org/environment

Committed to helping youth from around the world tackle global challenges.

# FURTHER READING


Clinton, Chelsea. *It's Your World: Get Informed, Get Inspired & Get Going!* New York: Philomel Books, 2015.

Espejo, Roman. *Adaptation and Climate Change.* San Diego: Greenhaven Press, 2012.

Fleischman, Paul. *Eyes Wide Open: Going Behind the Environmental Headlines.* Somerville, MA: Candlewick, 2014.

Klein, Naomi. *This Changes Everything: Capitalism vs. the Climate.* New York: Simon & Schuster, 2015.

Marcovitz, Hal. *What is the Future of Fossil Fuels?* San Diego: ReferencePoint Press, 2014.

# INDEX